Coastal LIVING

Coastal LIVING

A CELEBRATION OF LIVING BY THE WATER

HENRIETTA HEALD

RYLAND PETERS & SMALL
LONDON • NEW YORK

Senior designer Toni Kay
Commissioning editor Annabel Morgan
Location research Christina Borsi
Production manager Gordana Simakovic
Art director Leslie Harrington
Editorial director Julia Charles
Publisher Cindy Richards

First published in 2016
by Ryland Peters & Small
20–21 Jockey's Fields,
London WC1R 4BW
and
519 Broadway, 5th Floor
New York, NY 10012
www.rylandpeters.com

10 9 8 7 6 5 4 3 2 1

ISBN 978 1 84975 733 1

A catalogue record for this book is
available from the British Library.

US Library of Congress cataloging-in-
publication data has been applied for.

Printed and bound in China

Contents

Introduction

There is something magical about living by the water. Waking up to the call of
gulls and the crashing of waves on the shore brings you closer to the natural
world. If you live near a harbour, you may be lulled by the repetitive clink of the
wind in the rigging or the voices of fishermen as they land their catch in the early
morning. Even if you live in a remote spot, far from the bustle of a busy port,
there are constant reminders of nature and the power of the elements, whether
it is the intense heat of the midday sun or the ferocious winds that sweep over
the land during the hurricane season.

The architecture of many of the properties featured in this book has been
influenced by their coastal location. Cary Tamarkin designed his house on Shelter
Island with a wide 'breezeway' separating the living and sleeping areas so that
people experience direct contact with the elements every time they move
between the two. In Denmark, Birgitte and Henrik Møller Kastrup have a home
on the island of Funen where they stay all year round, so good insulation, a wood-
burning stove and cosy sheepskins are a vital part of the mix. On a warmer note,

India Hicks and David Flint Wood have created a paradise home on Harbour Island in the Bahamas, where shady verandahs, overhanging palm trees and whirring ceiling fans help them keep cool in the relentless heat.

The destructive potential of the elements is never far from the minds of coast-dwellers. Marta Nowicka's coastguard cottage in Sussex is testament to the danger of shipwrecks on England's South Coast, but even more poignant is the presence on Nantucket of 'widow's walks' – railed platforms where mariners' wives would await their husbands' return after a storm at sea.

In spite of the challenges, the owners whose homes are featured in this book share a passion for life by the ocean that is reflected in their choice of interior décor, from the intense blues and whites seen in Alex and Andrew Bates' home on Fire Island to the maritime artefacts on show at Jan Constantine's Cornish fisherman's cottage. In addition to showcasing this fabulous array of seaside homes, this book includes a wide range of delicious recipes and a series of illuminating articles on themes as varied as lighthouses, surfing, decorating with beach finds and plants for coastal gardens.

Henrietta Heald

CLASSIC COASTAL

ABOVE Fishing memorabilia is on display both inside and outside. Here, a length of sturdy rope has been coiled around a pair of wooden stanchions to make an unusual artwork.

ABOVE Jan's distinctive and popular soft-furnishing designs add vivid splashes of colour to every room in the house.

[handwritten annotations: "Should we think about making outside white" "Stay original" "idea" "like that color door maybe" "front porch" "the siding want"]

A Cornish fisherman's cottage

The ancient village of Port Isaac, situated close to the Camel Estuary in North Cornwall, is a source of endless inspiration to the designer Jan Constantine, who has owned a cottage there since 2001. The stone core of the building is believed to date from the 17th century and has provided a home for many generations of fishing families. Its original plan – two rooms on the ground floor and two rooms above, delineated by exceptionally thick walls – was simplicity itself. The entrance lintel is very low. 'People must have been much smaller in the days when it was built,' says Jan.

Sea Cove Cottage is perched on cliffs with a spectacular view across the tiny bay and beach, where there is always something interesting going on. In recent years, Port Isaac has been the main location for the television series *Doc Martin*, which featured Jan's cottage as the home of the character Louisa. The popularity of the series has attracted many tourists – with coffee shops and art galleries taking over from traditional food outlets and antiques stores – but Port Isaac is still an active fishing village, famed for its wonderful crab, and the place has not changed in other respects. 'The singing fishermen still sing on the beach on Friday evenings in summer, and the local brass band still plays too,' says Jan.

Although the old cottage had been converted into a holiday home in the 1960s, Jan knew when she bought it that the building needed a total

ABOVE This unassuming blue door flanked by terracotta pots has become an attraction for fans of *Doc Martin*, who flock to Port Isaac to find the locations used in the television series. The upper half of the façade is hung with tiles of Cornish slate in the traditional manner.

OPPOSITE It was very important to Jan and her family that the 17th-century cottage should retain its authentic appearance. Missing original features were replaced by modern lookalikes, such as the Cornish slate flags in the kitchen, where a Belfast sink and a blue Smeg refrigerator enhance the period feel.

13

THIS PAGE Enlivening an otherwise monochrome scheme, two of Jan's signature design motifs adorn the cushions on the living-room sofa: the British Union flag and heart shapes from her Love collection. Family connections with the sea are recalled in poignant images of sailors and in sailors' uniforms displayed behind glass.

makeover. There was a flat-roofed, 'L'-shaped extension containing the kitchen, with a large sink blocking most of the view, and a narrow sun room on one side. 'It all had to go!' says Jan. A full-width living room was added at the back and an open-plan kitchen area was set into the middle of the house. 'It took a lot of time and patience but eventually we got permission to extend the building, lifting the roof to create a more interesting apex with exposed beams. By installing a wall of glass doors to span the width of the cottage, we opened up the sea view.'

Despite the amount of work that proved necessary – including damp-proofing and installing new bathrooms on both floors – it was important to Jan and her husband David to retain the integrity of the building. New flagstones were sourced to match the original flooring and oak floors were laid elsewhere. Outside, the small area overlooking the harbour was paved and a half-height glass screen was erected at the seaward end of the terrace. 'This view is only for those with a good head for heights,' says Jan, 'especially now that we have exchanged our old iron balustrade for glass.'

A wooden bunk was built over the stairway to provide additional sleeping space and the original wooden panelling that survived in the back bedroom was repaired and later replicated in other rooms up to dado height.

THIS PAGE Most of the nautical items displayed on shelves and tables, including various pieces of shell jewellery and a ship in a bottle, were picked up at local junk shops. Some of the marine paintings hanging on the walls betray a nostalgia for the age of steam.

The interior decoration has been kept very simple, with plenty of white paint and touches of duck-egg blue. Many of the curtains are made of mattress ticking, but Jan used some of her embroidered seaside fabrics for curtains and blinds on the smaller windows. Most of the nautical artefacts on display in the cottage were found in local junk shops.

When the structural alterations were complete, Jan and David and their two young daughters started to spend as much time as they could at the cottage. In 2002 Jan set up a textile design business, which soon began to flourish, with homeware stores in Cornwall eager to stock her products, including cushions featuring seaside motifs such as fish, gulls and yachts. She has also supplied specially designed cushions to some of the leading hotels in the area.

Since her mother was a tailor and her grandmother a dressmaker, Jan believes that fabric design is in her blood. Over the years she has created an exquisite

OPPOSITE The textural contrast of roughly hewn stone and smooth wood panelling makes this wall an appealing backdrop for a collection of Cornish coastal scenes and lakeland images. A vertically propped fishing rod offers an interesting visual counterpoint to the horizontal lines of the picture frames.

ABOVE Suble tactile and visual juxtapositions add to the appeal of the table-top displays at Sea Cove Cottage. Here, a weathered slimline anchor is set at a jaunty angle against a windowsill, while neatly arranged items of fishing tackle are paired with smooth-surfaced shells and a jagged shell necklace.

RIGHT Jan Constantine's designs are inspired by her favourite things, particularly traditional embroidery. Images associated with the seaside, such as yachts, fish and gulls, are entirely at home in the cottage, but she also favours botanical and country garden themes, as well as emblems of love and patriotism.

collection of hand-embroidered textiles inspired by vintage and rural themes and her favourite things, including Union Flag designs. 'I like the Union Flag because I'm proud to be British and I sell hundreds of them, especially in London,' says Jan. Her soft furnishings are in great demand both in Britain and abroad; they range from the eye-catching bright colours of her Love collection to the more delicate traditional embroidery of hearts and flowers.

Sea Cove Cottage is now rented out to holidaymakers for most of the year, whenever it is not occupied by the family. And although Jan's main home is in Betley, near Crewe, 435 km/270 miles to the north, she still escapes to Cornwall whenever she can, especially during the quieter winter months, when the crowds of tourists have melted away. 'Life in Port Isaac is simple and relaxing.I find inspiration all around, so I book time in my diary to be here alone,'she says. 'Some of my best designs come to me at the seaside. Whenever I'm away, I can't wait to get back to the place.'

ABOVE Tongue-and-groove panelling, painted white, adds warmth to this old-fashioned bathroom with its chunky freestanding bathtub. Bathers like to linger in the tub so they can enjoy the panorama of hills across the tiny bay.

LEFT The guest bedroom, which looks out on the lane at the front of the house, has a single bed either side of the narrow window. The original wooden panelling was restored and replicated in other rooms up to dado height. A bold red, white and blue colour scheme gives this cosy space a patriotic feel.

OPPOSITE The most irresistible feature of Sea Cove Cottage is the paved terrace overlooking Port Isaac harbour, which is humming with activity for most of the year. Wood-framed, clear-glass panels were installed at the seaward end of the terrace to make the most of the views.

Dover sole, also known as common sole or black sole, combines a firm, succulent texture with a delicate but delicious flavour. The best and simplest way to cook it is *à la meunière*, a classic French method meaning 'in the style of a miller's wife' – a reference to the light dusting of flour given to the fish before cooking. You can either fry the fish in butter or, as here, bake it in the oven and make the butter-and-lemon sauce separately. The dark skin is traditionally removed before cooking.

Dover sole meunière

plain/all-purpose flour, for coating

sea salt

4 whole Dover sole (each about 500 g/18 oz.), skinned

vegetable oil, for cooking

250 g/2 sticks plus 2 tablespoons butter

freshly squeezed juice of 2 lemons

1 small bunch of fresh flat-leaf parsley, finely chopped

2 large baking sheets, greased and lined with baking parchment

Serves 4

Preheat the oven to 200°C (400°F) Gas 6.

Cover a large plate with flour and season with a little salt.

Drag the sole in the flour to lightly coat, then arrange on the prepared baking sheets. Drizzle with oil and rub all over to coat the fish.

Bake the fish in the preheated oven for 10 minutes. To test that the fish is cooked, insert a toothpick/cocktail stick into the thickest part of the fish – if the flesh is soft, the fish is cooked, but if it is still tough, then return to the oven for another couple of minutes and check again.

Meanwhile, make the sauce by melting the butter in a saucepan set over a medium heat – the butter will foam when it has melted as the water in the butter boils. As soon as the foaming has stopped the butter will start to cook. We then want the butter to cook for a while, until a distinctive nutty, hazelnut aroma is given off. Remove from the heat the moment this is achieved. Let the butter cool a little, then add the lemon juice and gently whisk together.

Reheat the sauce if necessary, but do not let it boil.

Serve the fish whole, covered generously with the sauce and a sprinkle of chopped parsley.

Coastal architecture

Houses by the sea come in all shapes and sizes, but the most impressive coastal architecture is designed in response to its surroundings, particularly to take advantage of panoramic views and to celebrate the majesty of nature.

Beach architecture reached its apotheosis in the 1930s and 1940s with the Art Deco craze in Miami Beach, characterized by nautical designs reminiscent of ocean liners, with wraparound verandahs and ziggurat (stepped) configurations. Early 20th-century Modernist architecture — with its emphasis on glass, steel, symmetry and white paint — was also well suited to

beachside locations, and influenced later generations in its celebration of buildings that make a bold statement.

Leading the way today are countries that revel in a year-round outdoor lifestyle, such as Australia, where beach houses have an expansive sense of space opening onto wide wooden decks. Often, all windows and doors are full-height glass. A similar, well-established trend is evident in Scandinavia, where, during the short but light-filled summer months, there is a desire to minimize distinctions between indoors and outdoors.

At the other end of the spectrum is the yearning for a more rural past evident in the clapboard and Colonial-style houses on the Eastern Seaboard of North America. A Mexico beach house consisting of huts modelled on native Mexican villages, with high roofs, or *palapas*, made from palms, exhibits a similar nostalgia. With their open sides capturing every passing breeze, and exposed to views of the ever-changing ocean, the *palapa* interiors are also an organic part of the outside world.

THIS PAGE The beautiful flower-and-leaf pattern etched into the kitchen units is unique. Devised by the innovative Copenhagen consultancy Design by Us, it enhances the subtle effects of sunlight and shadow.

Danish elegance

This tranquil home in Vedbaek, north of Copenhagen, is barely 50 metres (165 feet) from the beach, and on the landward side is a stream-filled forest, where the owners love to walk. Vedbaek came to world attention in 1975, when an important Mesolithic site was discovered there. By this time, the village was a popular retreat for wealthy Copenhagen families, who had begun building country homes in the area in the late 18th century. Several of these mansions still stand, adding a touch of grandeur to what is now a commuter suburb, only a short journey by car from the city centre. Although the fishing industry that once dominated the area has almost disappeared, many of the old mariners' cottages have been restored and modernized.

BELOW The exterior, which had been covered in a plastic paint, was the part of the house that needed the most work. It was stripped down to the bare bricks and re-covered with traditional stucco, while the upper storey was hung with slim wooden boards and painted dove grey.

RIGHT The beachy tones of the irregular sandstone floor tiles add a sense of underfoot warmth to this otherwise cool hallway. Here, as elsewhere in the house, French doors have been left wide open, tempting the visitor out into a brick-paved area that leads to the lush garden.

When Stine Langvad and her partner discovered the house in 2005, there was a great deal of work to be done – but Stine, who is an interior designer, positively relished the challenge. Built as a single-storey summerhouse in 1924, with an extension to the living area and an upper floor added a few years later, their new home consisted largely of a series of small, dark rooms.

They started by demolishing several internal walls, replacing the entire roof and building a brand new kitchen. Old carpets were removed to reveal the original floorboards, which were then sanded down and varnished. In typical Scandinavian style, the windows were left bare to admit as much daylight as possible. A striking modern fireplace was installed at mid-height in the new kitchen – one of the heating measures that has made it possible for the family to occupy the house all year round.

The ground floor now consists of a large, airy living area with adjoining office and a dining room with double doors to the kitchen.

LEFT A glass-fronted, armoire-style cupboard in one corner of the kitchen makes a perfect display case for a collection of drinking glasses, food-storage jars and clear-glass bottles.

BELOW A set of small leather suitcases, all similar in style and piled one on top of another, offers a practical form of storage, and makes an attractive alternative to shelves or bookcases.

Upstairs there is a master bedroom and a children's bedroom, one big bathroom and one shower room. The freestanding tub in the bathroom has been placed directly under a large window in the sloping roof, making for an exhilarating bathing experience.

On show in every room are Danish furniture classics, including works by Verner Panton, Arne Jacobsen and Poul Henningsen, combined with a harmonious mix of modern pieces. The walls in the living room are lined with deep bookshelves and cupboards. These were designed by Stine herself, but the period detailing on the front of the new cupboards gives the impression that they were built at the same time as the house.

'For me, the design and furnishing of an interior evolves over time,' says Stine. 'I don't start with a fixed idea about what should go where, but leave things to find their natural place.' She values pieces that are lovingly made and designed to last a lifetime. Occupying centre stage in the dining room is a Chinese black-lacquer table more than a century old. It was originally too high to go with the vintage Eiffel chairs by Charles and Ray Eames, so several inches were cut off the legs to make it fit.

The Copenhagen design consultancy Design by Us planned the kitchen in response to Stine's brief and devised the flower-and-leaf pattern etched into the white kitchen units, enhancing the subtle

THIS PAGE The Chinese black-lacquer table that dominates the dining room dates back to the early 19th century. Hanging over it is an antique candle-burning chandelier that makes a dramatic complement to the set of Eiffel chairs by Charles and Ray Eames and the minimalist modern painting above the old fireplace.

[handwritten annotation] every place window in back, put in french door?

effects of sunlight as it moves through the room during the course of a day. Sea-green tiles on the wall, made from Sicilian lava stone, have a rough surface that adds to the kitchen's rustic feel. Design by Us also crafted the long office desk specifically for the space it now occupies, and the office chair on castors is an Arne Jacobsen original. The office's clean lines and functional but stylish furniture make it one of the family's favourite rooms.

Stine's interest in design grew out of a basic need to tell stories and create spaces that draw people in. 'I'm simply attracted to beautiful objects, materials and

LEFT AND ABOVE Velvet cushion covers in jewel colours, a simple coffee table and an antique kelim are all that is needed to decorate the large living space, where most of the interest derives from the view through the French doors onto the verdant garden. Beyond the doors is a wide area of deck made of sustainable ipe wood. After dark, a few strategically placed floor and table lamps from the French company Jieldé provide artificial light in the living room. The plainly designed yet supremely comfortable sofas were acquired from the Italian furniture company Moroso.

ABOVE LEFT AND RIGHT Pieces of furniture that have seen better days, such as this paint-flaked chair, are used for display as well as functional purposes. Here, a few delicate flowers in a glass vase set on a small pile of books create a focal point in the corner of a room – a complement to the dramatic model yacht in the window. An antique knotted rug adds colour and interest to bleached floorboards.

works of art, and, without without being conscious of it, I always seem to end up with something that is distinctively "me".' Stine's beautiful objects are chosen for their function as well as their form and colour. 'There is no point putting a chair in a particular place simply because it looks good. If you don't also enjoy sitting in it – or using it as a surface for display – then there is no reason to have it there,' she says.

The exterior of the house was painted in what Stine calls 'the wrong sort of yellow plastic paint'. It had to be stripped down to the bare bricks and re-covered with traditional stucco, to which a white pigment had been added, which allows the bricks to breathe.

At the front of the living room are three pairs of French doors – which are left open when the weather permits – giving views onto the terrace and the garden beyond. For the terrace decking, the choice of material was ipe, an attractive hardwood that is both extremely durable and more sustainable than the alternatives.

The garden is a place of abundance and variety, and part of it has been left wild, which is how Stine likes it. A number of Mediterranean plant species, including olive trees, flourish there, together with jasmine, clematis and lavender.

OPPOSITE The renovations carried out by Stine and her partner over the past decade have made it possible for the house at Vedbaek to be occupied all year round. One of their more inspired moves was to install a modern fireplace at mid-height in the kitchen and build a store for logs underneath it. Among the family's favourite rituals in autumn is to roast chestnuts wrapped in foil on the open fire.

ABOVE LEFT Taking a bath under a big window is a marvellous way to feel closer to the natural world, especially in a room whose walls and floor are a soothing shade of sea green.

OPPOSITE With its clean lines and functional furniture, the office space is one of the family's favourite rooms. The chair is an Arne Jacobsen original. The desk was made specially for the room by Design by Us. Its yellow colour gives a real lift to the room, as well as apparently providing a stimulus to work. A selection of lively personal mementoes brightens up the wall.

ABOVE RIGHT In line with Scandinavian fashion, even in the bedrooms the windows are unobstructed by curtains or blinds, in order that as much light as possible can be admitted.

LEFT The veranda is a wonderful place to relax. Olive trees thrive in the garden here, along with thyme, jasmine, lavender, clematis and roses.

→ pots on in ground, I prefer in groove!

33

Nothing is more redolent of a warm summer evening on the beach than the aroma of fresh sardines or mackerel sizzling on an open barbecue. Marinading the oily fish in Campari and peaches gives this dish an Italian flourish, in which the bitterness of the liqueur acts as foil for the sweetness of the fruit. The peaches are grated rather than puréed, as in the classic Bellini cocktail, and some of the grated peach is mixed with thinly sliced fennel bulb and mint to make a piquant salad base for the fish.

Sardines with Campari, peach and fennel

6 sardines or 2 mackerel fillets

2 ripe peaches, stoned/pitted

2 tablespoons Campari

3 tablespoons olive oil

1 teaspoon sea salt

1 tablespoon peppercorn-sized breadcrumbs

1 handful of rustic croutons, made by toasting a piece of sourdough and ripping it into small pieces

1 fennel bulb, cut into thin strips, fennel tops reserved

1 handful of fresh mint leaves

1 teaspoon freshly ground black pepper

1 handful of black olives, stoned/pitted

Serves 2

If using sardines, butterfly them: remove the heads, trim the fins and slit the fish open from the belly down to the tail. Open the fish out like a book and place, skin-side up, on a board. Press down with your hand along the backbone to flatten it. Turn the fish over and pull out the backbone, cutting off the tail. Finally, pick out any obvious bones left behind.

Finely grate one of the peaches into a bowl and add the Campari. Set half this mixture aside in another bowl. Marinate the fish in half the peach-Campari mixture for 20 minutes.

Heat a frying pan/skillet (or barbecue/grill) over a high heat. Add 1 tablespoon of the olive oil, the salt and a layer of breadcrumbs. This will help prevent the flesh of the fish from sticking. Cook the fish for 4 minutes on one side, until the flesh is opaque. Flip and cook for 2 minutes on the other side. Add the croutons to the pan to toast them further.

Slice the remaining peach into slivers. Mix them with the fennel, croutons, mint leaves and pepper. Whisk the reserved peach-Campari mixture with the remaining olive oil and sprinkle over the fennel salad. Toss to coat. Serve the fish fillets on top of the salad. Garnish with the reserved fennel tops and black olives.

THIS PAGE Outdoor spaces are treated as extensions of indoor spaces in this beautiful seaside home. Just outside the kitchen is an enclosed porch with table and chairs, where the owners like to have breakfast after their morning walk on the beach.

white on blue-lite velvets there now

interest in not this color

like

A Nantucket Island retreat

[handwritten note:] → how to furnish home" inyl this

The current owners of Wonoma Lodge had been visiting Nantucket for more than 15 years before they acquired a house on the island in 2006, but the fact that it took so long was not surprising. In 1975 the entire island was designated a National Historic Landmark District, with strict conservation guidelines, and historic homes there have since become so highly prized that they are rarely put up for sale. 'When Wonoma Lodge came on the market, we bought it in the first few minutes, without viewing,' according to one of the owners. The house had been named after a daughter of Wauwinet, the chief of the Wampanoag people who originally inhabited the island.

Wonoma Lodge stands at the northeast point of the island, near the village of Wauwinet. In the owner's words, 'Its location is unique because you have the ocean as your backyard, the harbour view from your front door and protected national seashore on the other side of the dunes.' To accommodate their two daughters and other guests, she and her husband later bought a neighbouring boathouse, which, like Wonoma, used to belong to the 19th-century inn at Wauwinet.

ABOVE A widow's walk has been built on the roof of Wonoma Lodge. Open viewing platforms of this kind are a common feature of old Nantucket homes.

RIGHT AND FAR RIGHT The wide deck at the back of the house is sheltered by a ridge of dunes from the beach beyond. A separate outdoor seating area on the eastern side of the house, which catches the morning sun, overlooks a footpath leading directly to the sandy shore.

Both houses – or cottages, as they are usually known on the island – have grey cedar-shingle façades and white-painted window frames, doors and balustrades, reflecting the traditional architectural style of Nantucket.

Some 50 km (30 miles) south of Cape Cod, Nantucket was once a centre of the whaling industry vividly evoked in Herman Melville's *Moby-Dick*, whose characters Captain Ahab and Starbuck are both from the island. The silting up of the harbour in the mid-19th century prevented large whaling ships from entering and leaving, and the centre of the industry moved elsewhere. After a disastrous fire in 1846 led many other residents to leave, Nantucket remained isolated and relatively undisturbed for more than a century.

LEFT AND ABOVE Classic Nantucket style is in evidence throughout the house, with tongue-and-groove walls, ceilings and floorboards all painted white to reflect the natural light. Many of the floors have been covered with several coats of high-gloss marine paint, a traditional Nantucket choice of finish that only improves with age.

OPPOSITE The furniture here is a mixture of locally sourced items that reflect the maritime history of the island and hand-finished wooden pieces made specially for the house. Decorative items include shells, pebbles and rope sculptures.

The island is home to the largest concentration of pre-Civil War houses in the United States, most of them painstakingly restored.

A distinctive feature of old Nantucket cottages is the 'widow's walk', an observation platform on the roof from where fishermen's wives would gaze out to sea as they waited – sometimes in vain – for the return of their husbands' boats. These decks offer wonderful views of the island and the ocean beyond. Wonoma Lodge, which dates from the 1930s, was built without a widow's walk, so the current owners decided to add one, complete with white-painted wooden balustrade. It is reached from the upper floor via an old ship's ladder and trapdoor.

During their first summer at Wonoma, the owners lived in the cottage as they had found it, to get a feel for the space. Gradually, however, every element of the

LEFT A old ship's ladder has been tucked into a corner of the upper storey to provide access to the trapdoor that opens onto the widow's walk. Beside it is a linen storage cupboard, which was custom-made to fit the space.

BELOW Dormer windows were added to the upstairs rooms to provide additional light and make the most of the wonderful views. The pair of wrought-iron beds in this guest bedroom have been dressed with locally made woven fabrics and antique quilts.

love lamp

ABOVE The Boathouse is graced with a façade of cedar shingles that closely resembles that of Wonoma Lodge. A boardwalk cuts through the marram grass to reach the front door.

RIGHT Muted colours and pale wood characterize the entrance to the Boathouse. The slatted wooden shutters are opened and closed by means of a central spindle.

interior was updated. They started by moving the kitchen to the front of the building with a line of windows overlooking the harbour. The original footprint of the house was retained, but the upper floor, which had been added in the 1990s, was reconfigured to accommodate an extra bedroom and bathroom, making three bedrooms and two bathrooms in all. A glass-paned door was inserted on the upper floor to give access to a new balcony.

For interior decoration, the owners drew inspiration from the blues, greens and sandy browns of the surrounding environment. On the advice of local interior designer Janet Kielley, they followed Nantucket tradition by painting the floors with several coats of high-gloss marine paint, a beautiful finish that improves with age.

The grey-shingled façade of the Boathouse is similar to that of Wonoma Lodge, but in this instance an existing widow's walk was removed to provide more accommodation without having to increase the original height of the building. Living areas, including a kitchen, were created on the upper floor, which opens onto a balcony with harbour views.

Distressed, chalky textures and soft, faded hues were used to decorate the rooms. The floors consist of varying widths of antique, white-oak boards. 'Each board was individually sanded to recall the charm of a well-worn, uneven floor,' says Janet. 'The technique used to create the mellowed-driftwood effect involves bleaching the wood, then buffing it with an oil-based soap finish.'

The joy of this Nantucket retreat derives more from location than living space. When the current owners are in residence, they spend virtually all their time in the open air. 'We treat our outdoor spaces as extensions of the indoor spaces,' says one of them. 'Off the kitchen there is an enclosed deck with potted herbs and flowers, table and chairs, where we have breakfast after morning walks on the beach.' Leading off the main living space is another deck for relaxing and sunbathing. 'Some days it is enough just to sit there reading a good book, with our two Scottie dogs dozing nearby, listening to the roar of the sea as high tide approaches.'

The owners are now in the process of restoring a third house, which is adjacent to the other cottages but quite different architecturally. An example of the classic late-18th-century 'saltbox' style once common throughout New England, it has two storeys at the front and one at the back, with many of the elements of an authentic Shaker home.

LEFT AND ABOVE Open shelving, rustic earthenware pottery, antique door furniture and an abundance of wood combine to create a farmhouse feel in the Boathouse kitchen. Vertical tongue-and-groove panelling has been used to cover the walls to dado height, while the ceiling and the rest of the walls are clad in whitewashed planks aligned horizontally.

OPPOSITE The owners wanted the two cottages to feel as if they had always been there and took care to reflect this when choosing beams, floorboards, cupboards and furniture. The Boathouse living area, which opens onto a balcony, has a cushioned banquette along one side of the dining table, while locally made chairs complete the arrangement.

43

OPPOSITE A traditional bobbin bed, discovered in an antiques shop on the island, has been embellished with a mixture of linen and woollen textiles. Roman blinds made from woven grass fabric were hung at the windows of this bedroom to make the space feel warmer.

LEFT White-painted shutters have been used on most of the windows, but a few were left bare to allow light to flood in.

LEFT AND BELOW Many objects with nautical associations were added to the rooms to enhance the sense of being in a boathouse. These include a set of vintage oars and a large wooden propeller tipped with oxidized zinc. Chunky linens, worn wood and nubbly jute rugs add interest to the living area.

Although *coquilles St Jacques* means simply 'scallops' in French, the phrase is also commonly used to describe the traditional French dish of scallops poached in white wine and served in the shell after being sprinkled with breadcrumbs and browned under the grill/broiler. This variation includes diced and julienned vegetables along with a rich sauce of Pernod, wine and cream. The sauce is spooned into the shell with the raw scallops and cooked vegetables, topped with a layer of pastry and baked briefly in the oven.

Scallops St Jacques

1 carrot, peeled

1 celery stalk

1 onion, peeled

1 garlic clove, peeled

10 g/¾ tablespoon butter

a tiny pinch of sea salt

100 ml/½ cup white wine

10 ml/2 teaspoons Pernod (or other aniseed-based spirit/liquor)

50 ml/3½ tablespoons double/heavy cream

4 large hand-dived scallops

150 g/5½ oz. ready-made puff pastry, defrosted if frozen

Plain/all-purpose flour, for dusting

1 egg, beaten

Serves 4

This recipe is all about perfect knife skills. Take your time and cut a dozen matchsticks of carrot, a dozen 4-mm/⅛-in. cubes of celery and a dozen 4-mm/⅛-in. squares of onion. Slice the garlic clove into 8 very thin slices.

Put all the vegetable pieces and garlic in a small pan set over a very gentle heat with the butter and salt. Melt the butter and warm the vegetables for 15–20 minutes (they should not sizzle in the pan but just slowly become cooked through and translucent). Add the white wine and Pernod and bring to a low simmer for about 5 minutes to boil off the alcohol, then add the cream and take off the heat. Set aside to cool.

Preheat the oven to 180°C (350°F) Gas 4.

Prepare the scallops by removing the meat and the roe if it is a bright orange colour, then cleaning out the scallop shells. Set each element aside.

Roll out the pastry on a lightly floured work surface to a rectangle about 30 x 20 cm/12 x 8 in. and cut into 4 long strips.

Place 1 scallop with the roe, if using, 3 carrot sticks, 3 celery cubes, 3 onion pieces and 2 slices of garlic in each shell. Spoon over the sauce until the shell is two-thirds full. Place the top on the shell and paint the edge with the beaten egg before wrapping the edge with the pastry strip to seal. Finally, brush the pastry with the beaten egg. The scallops can be stored for up to 24 hours in the fridge at this stage.

Place the scallops on a baking sheet, using a little crumpled foil as a base to stop them from rolling around. Bake in the preheated oven for 12 minutes. Remove the scallops and rest for a few minutes before serving. Use some seaweed to support the shells on the plate.

To the lighthouse

If you live near a coastal waterway, you are never far from a lighthouse. Indeed, lighthouses have been an integral part of seaside topography for hundreds of years. Designed as aids to navigation, they must be conspicuous, so they are often sited on small islands or promontories, or even on rocks far out at sea. Many are painted bright white or boldly striped, making them even harder to miss.

As symbols of stability amid drama and potential danger, lighthouses have long fascinated writers and artists. In her novel *To the Lighthouse*, Virginia Woolf evokes an elusive destination, a goal that – although it seems near – is unattainable. The painter Edward Hopper immortalized a building on a rocky bluff in Cape Elizabeth, Maine, as an icon of loneliness and longing. Artists have also been prompted to illustrate the story of Grace Darling, the lighthouse-keeper's daughter who in 1838 rescued nine drowning men from a wreck on the Farne Islands, off the northeast coast of England.

The oldest lighthouse in the world still in use is the Roman-built Tower of Hercules in La Coruña, northwestern Spain. It was one of many buildings inspired by Pharos, the great lighthouse of Alexandria, which, at 150 metres (492 feet) high, was one of the Seven Wonders of the Ancient World.

Among the handful of lighthouses still open to visitors are the historic Cape Florida Light at Key Biscayne and Calcanhar in Brazil, which alerts ships to a coral reef 7 km (4.3 miles) offshore.

LEFT AND BELOW Hibiscus Hill on Harbour Island is the home of India Hicks and David Flint Wood, a couple who share a strong aesthetic sense and a passion for creating beautiful buildings. Since settling on the island more than 20 years ago, they have commissioned two more spectacular homes – the Guest House and the Cricket Pavilion – and overseen every aspect of the building and interior design process. While Hibiscus Hill remains India and David's family home, the other two houses are sometimes available for rent.

LEFT AND BELOW Hibiscus Hill on Harbour Island is the home of India Hicks and David Flint Wood, a couple who share a strong aesthetic sense and a passion for creating beautiful buildings. Since settling on the island more than 20 years ago, they have commissioned two more spectacular homes – the Guest House and the Cricket Pavilion – and overseen every aspect of the building and interior design process. While Hibiscus Hill remains India and David's family home, the other two houses are sometimes available for rent.

OPPOSITE The Guest House, completed in 1999, is built in the style of a Caribbean plantation house and set in a grove of coconut trees. On each of its two storeys is a wraparound veranda with views of pink-sand beaches and the turquoise ocean beyond.

Barefoot in the Bahamas

India Hicks and David Flint Wood made their home on Harbour Island in the Bahamas more than 20 years ago and now wouldn't live anywhere else, even though they maintain strong links with their native England. India is the daughter of David Hicks, the celebrated interior designer, who built a holiday house for himself and his family on Windermere Island in the 1960s. Savannah, as the house is called, was completed in 1967, the year of India's birth. Her mother is Lady Pamela Hicks, the daughter of Earl Mountbatten of Burma.

David Flint Wood arrived on Harbour Island on a boat from Nassau in the mid-1980s. He loved it so much that he gave up his career in advertising and started running a small hotel there. A few years later, India, whom he had met briefly before, turned up unexpectedly. 'She'd been staying with her parents on Windermere and had come to this virtually deserted island for some scuba diving,' says David. They had what he calls 'a *Casablanca* moment' – and the rest is history.

Soon afterwards, David and India bought Hibiscus Hill, a lovely old house overlooking the pellucid turquoise ocean and a beach of pink sand – a perfect place to 'live the dream' and raise a family. 'Our four children and foster son grew up there,' says David, 'and spent their childhood climbing trees and chasing snakes.' India expresses her love of the island, and her passion for healthy exercise, by running barefoot on the beach every day with her dogs.

Quite early on, as word of this tropical paradise spread among relatives and friends, David and India realized the need for a guest house, where visitors could stay for as long as they wished. Both of them have a strong sense of design and they had a very clear idea of what they wanted. 'New buildings were going up on the island by that time, but the prominent style was ersatz Florida Colonial,' says David. 'We wanted a house that looked like it had always been there.' They took on a highly experienced local architect, Henry Melich from Nassau, and employed local carpenters

THIS PAGE The cool, colonial feel of white-painted tongue-and-groove walls is enhanced by a central ceiling fan, a large potted palm and black-and-white photographs artfully arranged on a wall. The French doors lead straight onto the terrace, which wraps around the house on all four sides.

and craftsmen whose average age was 26, most of whom had never built anything before, but the result was a triumph.

The Guest House is a two-storey edifice in the style of an old Caribbean plantation house, set in a grove of coconut trees. On each level is a long verandah overlooking the beach. 'The beauty of the design is its modular simplicity,' explains David. There is a living area in the middle, flanked either side by two bedrooms and two bathrooms. All four bedrooms have wooden four-poster beds. The kitchen is sited in an extension at the back that local people call a 'lean-me-to'. A private path leads from the house to the beach. The Guest House was completed in 1999, six weeks before the arrival of Hurricane Floyd. Miraculously, even though the wind reached speeds of more than 260 kmph (160 mph), no damage was done to the house.

ABOVE A regimented arrangement of objects can work well in certain circumstances, as long as the items on show reflect the overall design scheme. Here, the juxtaposition of identical shapes creates an arresting pattern.

OPPOSITE In a corner of the Guest House, an amazing number of disparate objects have been assembled to create a three-dimensional mixed-media 'scrap wall'. Images of boats, animals and plants jostle for space with photographs of Caribbean scenes and individuals. The open-fronted cabinet makes an ideal display case for shells of all shapes and sizes, and other objects with nautical associations are lined up along the top of the wood and rattan desk. This apparently chaotic arrangement is in reality carefully thought out and designed to have a soothing effect on the observer.

ABOVE LEFT AND RIGHT The simple pencil bed and side table in a Guest House bedroom were designed by David Flint Wood and made by hand on the island. At the head of the bed, the graceful sweep of a pair of feather-light curtains frames a striking painting in an oval frame. Otherwise, the look is clean and uncluttered, except for a few shells on the bedside table.

RIGHT A plain white bathing space is enlivened by quirky items such as a mirror with shutters and a decorative wrought-iron chair. The floorboards are stained dark brown to match the door.

Classic Coastal

Spurred on by the success of their first building venture, David and India went on to create the Cricket Pavilion, a single-story studio that from the outside resembles a piece of Neoclassical English architecture. The idea of the pavilion came from a love of cricket. 'I used to play the game on the road with my son and the artist Anish Kapoor, his godfather. It was very competitive,' says David. 'Then one day India said, "We should build a club house." We found a model for it on the nearby island of Eleuthera.'

The Cricket Pavilion is essentially a wood-framed modular cube surrounded by a broad terrace. The interior consists of a huge open-plan living area and kitchen with a vaulted ceiling rising to a cupola and white-painted wooden floorboards. There are two large

THIS PAGE Louvred shutters control light flow in living areas with many windows, while a heavy table, a vintage globe and some weighty books anchor the scheme.

ABOVE The outside and inside of the Cricket Pavilion are quite different from each other. The exterior is meant to replicate certain elements of English Neoclassical architecture, while the interior is essentially a huge, open-plan living area with a vaulted ceiling. There are two bedrooms and bathrooms at the back. Walls, floors and ceilings are painted white, and most of the rooms, including the terrace, are cooled by ceiling fans.

RIGHT Light streaming through a window between a pair of floor-to-ceiling bookcases in the living room clearly illustrates why this piece of furniture by Philippe Starck is called a Ghost chair.

BELOW The proper appreciation of outdoor living in the Bahamas and other parts of the Caribbean depends on overhanging roofs that provide protection from tropical downpours as well as from the intense heat of the sun.

bedrooms with their own bathrooms in the back half. 'It resembles a modern apartment that you might find in New York, Paris or London,' says David. 'Then you look out of the window and see a scene from a painting by Gauguin or Matisse, with coconut trees and palms.'

David regrets the fact that most building materials, including the cedar shingles used for roofing, have to be imported into the Bahamas. 'There was once abaco pine here, but it's all gone.' He and India encourage the hand-making of furniture on the island. 'We even had a makeshift bed factory to make pencil beds, which were hand-sanded.' Local craftsmen also make dining tables and side tables.

India set up a business on Harbour Island based on the Spiderlily fragrance she created for Crabtree & Evelyn. She now makes and markets her own collection of luxurious bath and body products and accessories under the brand name India Hicks London–Harbour Island. David's expertise in architecture and interior design is much in demand on the island and further afield. Among other achievements, he has decorated a house in New York for the actress Brooke Shields, which was featured on the cover of *Architectural Digest*.

ABOVE The Cricket Pavilion has a long, broad terrace and an oblique view of the ocean. The interior is completely modern in design, with white-painted floorboards and a mixture of modern and antique furniture and artwork.

RIGHT The dramatic scale of this exotic birdcage is emphasized by the dark wooden chairs on either side.

OPPOSITE David and India have combined antique and new pieces to intriguing effect in the Long Room of their Cricket Pavilion. A small still-life oil painting hangs behind an 18th-century gilded chair, and vintage white tennis balls are displayed in the form of a modern artwork. The successful pairing of disparate items depends on achieving a harmony of tone.

You may like to eat your oysters raw, served on the half-shell with a little lemon juice and black pepper or a dash of Tabasco, but they can be equally delicious poached, steamed, grilled or browned in a hot oven. In this version, the oysters are steamed upright in their shells after being doused in lemony white wine and dotted with cream. They need only a few minutes cooking time – take care not to overcook them or the meat will become chewy. Serve three oysters each with bread and butter for an elegant starter, or one each as a canapé.

Poached oysters

6 oysters, shucked

1 tablespoon crème fraîche or double/heavy cream

1 tablespoon dry white wine

1 tablespoon grated lemon zest

2 tablespoons shaved fennel

1 teaspoon fennel tops

1 tablespoon flaked/slivered almonds, toasted

freshly ground black pepper

sourdough bread and butter, to serve

steamer with a lid

Serves 2 as a starter/appetizer with drinks

Pour off some of the oysters' natural juices. Layer the shells so that they stay upright in a steamer basket.

Carefully dot the oysters with the crème fraîche or cream and drizzle with the white wine and lemon zest.

Bring the water under the oysters to a medium simmer and put the lid on the steamer. Steam the oysters for 5–7 minutes.

Top with the shaved fennel, fennel tops and toasted almonds and season well with black pepper.

Serve with good sourdough bread and butter.

MODERN COASTAL

FAR LEFT The glass-fronted 'box' with its uninterrupted views of beach and ocean seems to hover just above the sand dunes. Two sun-bleached Adirondack chairs keep each other company on the private beach.

LEFT The 4-metre (13-foot) overhang at the back of the house creates plenty of room for a sheltered car port. From here, there is access to the beach along a secluded path through the dunes.

Shooting the breeze on Shelter Island

Cary Tamarkin discovered the site of this wonderful house by chance – and at once seized the opportunity to buy it. Having had several vacations in the Hamptons as a child, he returned in 2005, in midwinter, to look for a waterfront home of his own. While there, he was tipped off about a property that had just become available on Shelter Island, a tranquil enclave located between the north and south forks of Long Island. Cary had never visited the island before, even though it was just a five-minute ferry ride from Sag Harbor, a place he knew well.

RIGHT Just visible through the indigo-painted door is the dining space, which forms part of the large, open-plan living room. There is direct access to the living area from the breezeway, where the old-growth cypress cladding has weathered to a pale silver colour.

THIS PAGE In Cary's opinion, the real triumph of the house is its breezeway, flanked on one side by the living area and on the other by the sleeping area. People moving from one part to the other must cross an open area 3.7 metres (12 feet) wide, bringing them into contact with the natural elements. A slatted roof provides a combination of sun and shade.

The building that occupied the site when Cary bought it was an old shack from the 1960s, which had no insulation and was hardly habitable. Nevertheless he and his partner decided to live there for a while, to get a real feel for the location and the kind of house that would suit it best.

Cary is an architect and he knew that, as well as drawing up viable plans, he would have to get various environmental permits for building close to the water. In the event, the process took three years – but it was so valuable that Cary came to wonder how any architect could really understand a location without living there for a while.

'It's an amazing site, facing southwest, so you get a gentle breeze all summer and gorgeous sunsets,' he says. 'You feel as if you're on your own, with wide open spaces in both directions.' The only other dwelling visible from the house belongs to their neighbour to the southeast, a painter and composer who has a small studio. 'The whole island is very artistic,' says Cary.

The new house was built on the same footprint as the original, but a 4-metre (13-foot) overhang was added at each end to extend the interior space dramatically.

OPPOSITE The open-plan kitchen, dining and living space has floor-to-ceiling windows and doors leading to the large deck overlooking the beach. A variety of seating breaks up the space without enclosing it.

LEFT This classic Hans Wegner Lounge chair, dating from the early 1950s, has a pale oak frame, a woven rush seat and angled back.

ABOVE Interior walls and ceilings are lined with oiled cedar panelling, while concrete is the material used for floors, kitchen counters and the fireplace surround. A quartet of Hans Wegner Lounge chairs has been arranged around a circular, marble-topped coffee table. These are just a handful of examples of Cary Tamarkin's fine collection of mid-20th-century furniture.

The house is effectively raised on a platform about 3 metres (9–10 feet) above the ground. At the front there are steps up to a breezeway and a big front porch where the Tamarkins and their guests spend most of their time in summer.

'It is a big box divided in three,' explains Cary. 'There's a sleeping porch and a living porch separated by the breezeway.' The breezeway – a large roofed deck open to the elements – is regarded by Cary as the best part of the whole design. The distance of 3.7 metres (12 feet) between sleeping quarters and living quarters means that, whatever the weather, residents are thrown into close contact with nature.

Almost the entire house, both inside and out, is made of wood. The main building material is old-growth cypress that has spent 100 years submerged in the bogs of Georgia and Florida. This works well in a waterside setting because it is rot-resistant. Some of the massive beams used in the construction are up to 9 metres (30 feet) long. Floors are concrete, with radiant heating beneath for the cooler months of the year.

'I wanted a cabin, and this house has the attitude of a cabin,' says Cary. 'I like to pare back and back.' He describes himself as both an architect and a developer, working mostly on residential buildings in Manhattan, and occasionally detached country houses, but he is selective about the projects he takes on because he finds that houses are more time-consuming to get right, and consequently less profitable.

ABOVE The main deck runs the entire length of the living space, with ocean views on one side and floor-to-ceiling glass doors on the other. The teak dining tables and bench seats have weathered to the same pale grey colour as the cypress floorboards.

OPPOSITE A walnut-topped Eero Saarinen Tulip table is flanked by a set of Hans Wegner CH33T chairs, used for dining rather than relaxing. Floor-to-ceiling windows blur the boundary between indoors and out.

THIS PICTURE A fabulous covered terrace, with views over the bay to the south fork of Long Island, is the perfect place for guests to gather and make plans for the day. The only other building visible from this shady haven is an artist's studio belonging to the Tamarkins' neighbour.

ABOVE Shelter Island is linked to Sag Harbor on Long Island by a small car ferry that runs every 10 or 15 minutes. The brief journey can also be made by private boat to the beach in front of the house, where there is a jetty for mooring. At high tide, the jetty appears to float in the ocean.

'When you want to create a work of art, as we've done here, it is a labour of love.'

Cary had collaborated on several projects with the interior designer Suzanne Shaker and he asked her to take responsibility for the interior furnishings, which combine warm colours and natural fibres. Lighting has been kept to a minimum so as not to detract from the effect of the night sky. Paper lamps by Isamu Noguchi and other discreet task-lighting enhance the subtle gleam of the cypress wood.

There are five bedrooms, all built on the ocean side of the house, within earshot of the waves. In addition, there are plenty of other places to sleep, such as comfortable sofas, which means that 16–20 people can be accommodated there.

'My girlfriend really loves to cook and entertain. She loves it when lots of people come over,' says Cary. 'And there's nothing

that I like better than hanging out on the porch, playing the guitar and the mandolin with my friends, many of whom are musicians.'

In front of the house is a great sweep of beach, which, although private, is free for anyone to use. Like much of the rest of Shelter Island, the landscape has been left almost untouched. Nearly one-third of the island, including vast tracts of wetland, is owned by the Nature Conservancy to be preserved in a wild state. There are four nature- and bird-watching trails, and the island has provided locations for several films and television series.

LEFT The small deck that leads off the master bedroom provides space for a simple, wood-lined outdoor shower. It was designed within the rectangular footprint of the house and is open to the sky above and the ocean in front.

ABOVE LEFT Built-in beds double as seating in a child's bedroom. Possibly influenced by the compact style of boat interiors, the Tamarkins have chosen quite a few examples of built-in furniture for their island home.

ABOVE RIGHT A glass ceiling in an ensuite bathroom allows natural light to flood into the shower cubicle during the day and offers great views of the stars at night.

OPPOSITE This tranquil master bedroom is sited on the seaward side of the house, so that its occupants wake up to the sound of waves lapping the shore.

Reflecting the vibrant colours of the Spanish flag, this variation on
a traditional Lenten dish uses smoked haddock rather than salt cod.

Catalan rice with chickpeas, smoked haddock and red pepper

300 g/10 oz. undyed smoked
haddock fillet

250 g/1¼ cups cooked, soaked
dried chickpeas/garbanzo beans
or the contents of 1 x 400-g/14-oz.
can, drained

a generous pinch of saffron
strands

1 red (bell) pepper

2 large tomatoes

3 tablespoons olive oil

6 garlic cloves, finely chopped

250 g/1¼ cups short-grain rice,
such as Bomba

2 hard-boiled/cooked eggs,
peeled and cut into quarters

Serves 4

Poach the smoked haddock gently in water for about 5 minutes, until it flakes
easily, and then drain. Flake the fish with a fork, removing any stray bones and
skin, and set aside.

Preheat the grill/broiler.

Warm the chickpeas/garbanzo beans in a little water, crumbling the strands
of saffron lightly with your fingers into the pan. Simmer very gently for about
20 minutes, during which time they will take on the colour and flavour of the
saffron. Drain through a sieve/strainer, reserving the golden cooking water,
and set both aside.

Cut the red (bell) pepper in half lengthways, remove the stalk and seeds and
put the 2 halves under the preheated grill/broiler, skin-side up, until the skins
blacken. Put the pepper into a plastic bag for a few minutes, then lift off the
blackened skins and slice the 2 halves into thin strips.

Either blanch the tomatoes in boiling water for 1 minute, peel, deseed and chop
the pulp, or cut in half crossways, scrape out the seeds and grate the cut side of
each half into a shallow bowl, leaving the skin behind. This is the Catalan way of
doing it; they even grow special varieties of tomato for grating, with tough skins.

Heat the olive oil in a pan and cook the garlic gently for 1–2 minutes, until it
becomes golden and ceases to smell of raw garlic. Be careful not to burn it. Add
the tomato pulp and cook for another 5 minutes or so, until it has disintegrated,
and then tip the rice into the pan and stir around thoroughly until every grain
is coated. Add 600 ml/2½ cups water, including the saffron-flavoured golden
cooking water, and bring to the boil. Simmer for 20 minutes, uncovered, until
the rice is cooked and no liquid remains. Adjust the seasoning, bearing in mind
that the smoked fish is already quite salty.

Stir in the chickpeas/garbanzo beans and flaked fish, heat through for a
few minutes, then strew the strips of red (bell) pepper over. Place the hard-
boiled/cooked egg quarters on top of everything. Keep in a warm place
for 10 minutes for the flavours to meld together, then serve.

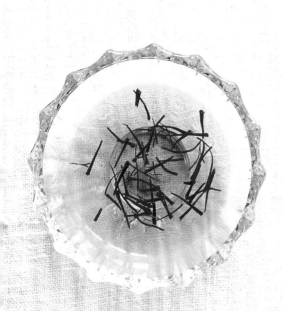

Catching the perfect wave

From Byron Bay in Australia to Newquay in Cornwall, surfers regard surfing as not only the ultimate watersport but also a transcendental experience that allows them to merge more fully with nature than any other activity.

Riding the waves originated in ancient Polynesia, where it was an integral part of the culture. Both male and female surfers were observed in Tahiti in 1769 by Joseph Banks, a botanist travelling with Captain James Cook, who noted that prowess in the surf determined a person's social standing.

Surfing really took off in the early 20th century, when the focus moved from Hawaii to California. It is now a professional sport with millions of followers, some addicted to the thrill of danger.

Today, dedicated surfers travel huge distances in search of 'the perfect wave' – which may be anything up to 30 metres (100 feet) high. Increasingly sophisticated wetsuits have made the sport possible in colder waters, such as off the coast of Scotland, but also as far north as Iceland, where particularly brave souls surf among the icebergs.

For many surfers, their sport is a way of life with its very own 'surf lingo'. A 'beach break', for example, is a wave that breaks on the sandy seabed – the best type for beginners. A 'reef break', on the other hand, is one that breaks over a coral reef or a rocky seabed, while a 'point break' breaks onto a rocky promontory. The latter gave its name to *Point Break*, a film released in 1991 directed by Kathryn Bigelow and starring Patrick Swayze and Keanu Reeves.

LEFT The design and orientation of a Modernist beach house on the south fork of Long Island make the most of the breathtaking ocean views. The fragility of the ecosystem associated with the dunes means that building on this spot would not be allowed today.

THIS PICTURE Cedar shingles are one of the most popular building materials for coastal homes in this part of the USA. Over time, through the action of salt, wind and sun, the cedar wood weathers to a soft silver.

Surfside in the Hamptons

This beguiling seaside home occupies a prime site in the fashionable resort of Bridgehampton on the south fork of Long Island. Dating originally from the 1970s, Surfside is described by Stelle Architects – who restored and remodelled it for a Hollywood film producer and his Swedish wife – as 'a simple rectangular pavilion clinging to the dunes where water meets land'. Enormous expanses of glass on the seaward side offer exhilarating views of the beach and the ocean beyond.

'You wouldn't be allowed to build here now since it's too close to the water,' says Eleanor Donnelly of Stelle Architects, who have designed similar buildings in the area. The fragile ecosystem based on the dunes where the house stands makes it a sensitive area for nature conservation. Fear of floods during the hurricane season prompted the architects to incorporate a 'breakaway' device, whereby the lower section of the house will break away if flooding occurs, protecting the rest of it. The master bedroom and bathroom are located on the upper level and electrical panels are installed well off the ground.

The renovations were done in two stages, with the first stage carried out over several weeks to get the house ready for a family event on Memorial Day weekend. The second stage took nine months. The owners are based in Los Angeles but have other houses in different parts

of the world, including an apartment overlooking Central Park in New York, so they spend only a short period of the year at Surfside – not much more than the eight weeks of summer. When they do visit, they like to feel immediately at home and relaxed, with no worries about causing damage or walking through the house with sandy feet, so they commissioned Stelle to create an interior that was functional and unpretentious.

'This is truly a beach house, not a museum piece that's never used,' says Eleanor Donnelly, who was involved in the restoration project. 'The grey tones in much of the interior were chosen deliberately so that they wouldn't distract attention from the dramatic seascapes and what's going on outside.' The main building material consists of grey cedar planks, which are attached to the inside and the outside of an interior frame. These age to a silky silver colour.

ABOVE LEFT AND RIGHT A wide wooden terrace supported by concrete pillars runs along the entire seaward side of the house. There are smaller decked areas at the back, reached from the inside by means of floor-to-ceiling glass doors and from below by an outdoor staircase.

OPPOSITE Stelle Architects' first major modification was to create in the centre of the building a Scandinavian-style, open-plan kitchen with sliding doors to the terrace. They did this by taking out a fireplace that had formed a barrier between the kitchen and the living room. The sleek counters are made of ApplePly.

In the first stage of the renovation work, the architects removed an interior chimney and installed a new kitchen, which is now the centrepiece of the home. The owners are very sociable and passionate about cooking, so they wanted a big open-plan space, Scandinavian in style, where they could entertain their numerous guests. A fireplace for spit-roasting was built inside the room but on an exterior wall, replacing a previous fireplace that had formed an obstacle between the kitchen and living room. The house's exposed location makes it too windy for outdoor barbecues.

The new kitchen surfaces are made of ApplePly, known for its attractive exposed edges that show the end grain of the wood panels. Countertops in the bathrooms and elsewhere consist of a beautiful dark-grey stone called basaltina.

Another major intervention by Stelle Architects was to install the huge window in the living area that reveals a long sweep of beach. So dramatic are the views from

ABOVE Pictures and other display items are few and far between in this comfortable but functional interior. All the objects on show in this simple arrangement have a practical as well as an aesthetic purpose.

OPPOSITE Light pours into the living room through a magnificent window installed by Stelle Architects. The dramatic coastal vistas framed by the window have led many observers to believe that they are looking at a work of art rather than a natural scene. A built-in bench with plump seat cushions runs the whole length of the wall.

BELOW An outdoor shower and sauna area leads off the breezeway, making it easily accessible to all guests. A light whitewash has been applied to the walls to blur the decorative distinctions between inside and outside. One of Stelle's later modifications was to add a steam room to what is now described as a 'sauna suite'.

this window that it is often mistaken for an artwork. Luxurious and comfortable banquette seating in this room runs for 6 metres (20 feet) along the wall, with capacious storage drawers underneath.

The second stage of the development of Surfside included expanding the sleeping accommodation for owners and guests, reconfiguring the living room and installing a deck for entertaining. The new guest spaces are designed to connect easily with the more 'public' spaces of the house, while maintaining privacy for the owners.

'Our goal was to keep the seaside spirit of this house alive in the architecture and finishes,' says Stelle. 'Simplicity in design, high-quality materials and responsible energy use were all high priorities for our clients.' Materials were chosen for their strength and durability against the salt-water environment and natural ventilation was maximized to limit the need for mechanical cooling. Photovoltaic cells, hot-water panels and geothermal heat pumps were installed to make the property self-sufficient in energy.

Interior finishes have also been kept simple and require very little maintenance. Colour palettes reflect the ocean tones and celebrate the similarities and differences between the beach and the land.

'We believe in a low-key, non-invasive and low-maintenance approach to both design and construction,' say the architects. 'Inspired by indigenous forms and materials, we strive to create environments that respect and celebrate the beauty and fragility of the natural landscape in which our buildings are sited.'

ABOVE AND OPPOSITE A simple divan/box spring bed accentuates the streamlined décor of the airy master bedroom, which opens directly onto the deck at the front of the house – an arrangement that was later modified by Stelle Architects to improve the owners' privacy. The bare expanse of plain wooden floors and white-on-white bed linen reinforce the minimalist look, while a built-in closet conceals everyday clutter. Shells on a beside table and a pile of books on the floor are the only decorative objects. The utilitarian floor lamp is inspired by Poul Henningsen.

THIS PAGE Making the most of a fabulous beachside setting depends on the good design of outdoor spaces. Discreetly sited decks and terraces can expand the sense of openness in a dwelling, while helping to define the architecture in relation to its natural surroundings.

OPPOSITE, ABOVE AND BELOW The sand dunes along this coast have suffered serious erosion in recent years, and flimsy wooden fences offer little protection, but the dunes are gradually being strengthened by the planting of marram grass, bayberry and other native species.

Many varieties of seafood – crab, squid, mussels, scallops – work well in summer salads, but in this recipe king prawns/jumbo shrimp play the starring role. When combined with finely sliced red chilli/chile, they make a brilliant match with a creamy avocado dressing that includes tangy lime, fresh coriander/cilantro and fromage frais or ricotta cheese.

Seafood salad with avocado dressing

4 handfuls of torn red Little Gem/Bibb lettuce

1 red (bell) pepper, deseeded and thinly sliced

50 g/2 oz. sugar snap peas, sliced diagonally

3 spring onions/scallions, thinly sliced diagonally

100 g/⅔ cup shelled fresh uncooked peas

350 g/12 oz. peeled and deveined cooked king prawns/jumbo shrimp

1 red chilli/chile, deseeded and finely sliced

Avocado dressing

2 avocados, peeled, halved, stoned/pitted and chopped

freshly squeezed juice of 2 limes

finely grated zest of 1 lime

6 tablespoons fromage frais or ricotta cheese

2 tablespoons freshly chopped coriander/cilantro leaves, plus extra to serve (optional)

½ teaspoon chilli flakes/dried hot red pepper flakes

sea salt and freshly ground black pepper

Serves 4

To make the avocado dressing, put all the ingredients in a blender and blend until smooth and creamy. Add a little water to loosen, if needed, and season well.

Arrange the lettuce leaves on a large serving plate, then top with the red (bell) pepper, sugar snap peas, spring onions/scallions, peas and king prawns/jumbo shrimp. Spoon the avocado dressing on top before sprinkling with the sliced chilli/chile and extra coriander/cilantro, if you like.

An exquisitely Danish escape

ABOVE The Møller Kastrup family are often to be found gathered around the table in the dining area. During the summer months, the doors are usually left wide open, connecting the inside with the exterior decked area. In winter, the log-burning stove provides efficient heating and the sheepskin throws help to make the space feel snug and cosy.

OPPOSITE The only parts of the house without views over the beach are the small kitchen and bathroom, which are located along the rear wall. Above these rooms is the mezzanine sleeping area.

Birgitte and Henrik Møller Kastrup bought this charming summerhouse on the Danish island of Funen in 2010, since when they have used it at every opportunity as a retreat from the stresses and pressures of modern city life. The couple's main home is in Kerteminde, 15 kilometres (10 miles) away, and they also own a houseboat on the Christianshavn canal in Copenhagen, but they spend all summer at this idyllic seaside escape, as well as weekends throughout the year.

When the owners are in residence, the house is often full of family and friends, which is exactly how they like it. 'It's important to us that our home is used as much as possible,' says Henrik. 'We relax there, we work there, we entertain there. We use it for all kinds of things.'

Funen is Denmark's second largest island, located between mainland Denmark and the island of Zealand. It is known as the country's garden island on account of its gently rolling hills, its orchards and hedgerows and its thatched, half-timbered farmhouses. The archipelago south of Funen incorporates many beautiful bays, straits and inlets, as well as islands of various sizes, linked to their larger neighbours – and each other – by bridges and ferry routes. There are also plenty of old castles and historic buildings to explore. Funen can be reached by car via the Little Belt Bridge

LEFT Chunky glass bottles are put on display and used to contain an arrangement of dried grasses. Their transparency adds to the light and airy feel of the living space. A collection of pebbles and shells adorns the shelf behind.

RIGHT Birgitte and Henrik share a fondness for antiques, including rustic earthenware pottery, and try to create visual surprises by pairing old and new items. Henrik has the largest collection in Denmark of old signs and posters with a dairy theme.

from the mainland and the Great Belt Bridge from Zealand. The largest city on the island is Odense, the birthplace of the author Hans Christian Andersen.

Although the Møller Kastrup home was completed as recently as 1998, it has the look and feel of a typical Danish summerhouse dating from the 1920s, the period when other houses were built along this coastline – houses that now form the basis of a thriving holiday resort. One thing that makes the building special is its underfloor heating system, which allows the house to be used throughout the year. In fact, Birgitte and Henrik love to come here for winter weekends, when they can spend hours curled up with good books in front of the log-burning stove. Most of the interior walls are clad in horizontal tongue-and-groove panelling, which offers insulation and textural warmth during the colder months.

Few alterations and additions were needed when the couple moved in because the house suited their needs

OPPOSITE The steeply pitched ceiling in the living area adds an exhilarating sense of light and space to this otherwise compact home. The soft periwinkle blue used to decorate the walls perfectly mimics the colours of the sea and sky, changing to a warm pebble grey as the light fades.

RIGHT An inviting rattan chair covered with a cosy sheepskin is carefully placed by the open French door, next to a lightweight vintage stool that doubles as a side table. This is the ideal place to relax and enjoy the summer breezes or to contemplate taking a walk on the beach.

BELOW The focal point of this corner is the set of three identically framed photographs of coastal scenes. Hanging them one under the other creates the illusion of an additional window. A streamlined modern sofa is the ideal seating choice for this spot.

RIGHT An enticing reading nook built into an alcove incorporates useful shelving. Underneath there is more storage in the shape of drawers on castors that can be pulled out for ease of use. The nautical chart displayed on the wall helps to root the building in its location.

OPPOSITE Making efficient use of the elevated roof space, Birgitte and Henrik have created a mezzanine level, accessed by a nautically inspired ladder. It adds architectural interest to the house, as well as providing a sleeping space for three people.

almost perfectly. 'We made some minor changes to the layout and altered the colour schemes in some of the rooms,' says Henrik. 'The most important thing we did was to insert four windows in the roof, allowing a great deal more light to penetrate into the top floor.'

During daytime hours, the entire house is awash with natural light and there is an apparently seamless connection between the outside and the inside. This effect is achieved by an abundance of glass – not only windows but also a series of double glass doors that open onto the wraparound terrace. In summer the doors to the terrace are usually left open, giving direct access to the pebble beach and the sea beyond.

Life is largely lived out of doors, when the weather permits, so the house and its wooden deck have been planned to allow residents to enjoy the seascape to the full. Inside, the high ceilings add to the sense of space, but the artful layout and design also combine to create an intimate feel. The only parts of the house that don't have views over the beach are the kitchen and bathroom, which are situated along the

OPPOSITE To create visual interest in this small bathroom, an elegantly carved wooden table has been painted white and modified to accommodate the plumbing for a countertop basin. The wall fixtures, including the mirror, are simple in style but stand out against a wall of multicoloured miniature tiles.

RIGHT AND BELOW The single conventional bedroom has a strongly nautical feel, with a small double bed that fits inside snugly, as in a ship's cabin. The sliding door, porthole-shaped mirrors and blue-grey colour scheme combine to reinforce the maritime aesthetic.

rear wall. Above these rooms is a mezzanine sleeping area, reached by a nautical-style ladder, that makes good use of the roof space.

Since there is only one conventional bedroom in this compact summerhouse, the mezzanine area is invaluable when it comes to putting up guests. 'The loft is big enough for three people to sleep there,' explains Henrik, 'and we can squeeze two more into the annexe, which is about 5 metres (16 feet) from the main house.' The couple's own bedroom, which is barely large enough to take more than a double bed, recalls a cosy boat's cabin – an effect echoed in a series of circular mirrors resembling portholes that have been carefully arranged on the walls.

The couple share a great fondness for antiques and they love to combine old and new items in their various homes. 'I have the largest collection in Denmark of old signs,' says Henrik, who has also amassed a collection of old posters with a dairy theme, reflecting a long-term involvement in his family's dairy business.

During Denmark's short winter days, the challenge is how to create a cosy atmosphere in this exposed coastal home and get warm again after bracing walks along the beach. To supplement the log-burner and underfloor heating, Birgitte and Henrik make good use of woollen textiles, particularly Scandinavian sheepskins, which are draped over many of the sofas and chairs.

ADMIRAL PENN
*One of Cromwell's Admirals who took
Jamaica from the Spaniards*
from the Original Picture
London Published by S. Woodburn, 1811

The story of rum

Dark and Stormy, Cox's Daiquiri, Rum Baba, Papa Hemingway... our modern experience of rum is largely confined to fabulous cocktails and exotic desserts. It is all too easy to forget that the spirit has a fascinating, centuries-old history.

Rum is distilled from molasses (dark rum) or sugar cane juice (white rum). There is no rum without sugar – and there is no part of the world more closely linked with rum than the Caribbean, where the first sugar mills were established in 1516. As sugar production increased, European colonialists imported slaves from Africa to work their plantations in Jamaica, Cuba and Puerto Rico.

LE SUCRE

English settlers in Barbados cultivated sugar cane from imported seeds, and locals began distilling a spirit from the dark, treacly molasses that remained from the sugar-refining process. It soon became extremely popular – and spread to other sugar-producing areas. A visitor to Barbados wrote, 'The chief fuddling they make on the island is Rumbullion... made of sugar canes distilled, a hot, hellish, and terrible liquor.'

When Jamaica was captured by the British in 1655, the invaders were introduced to the local spirit. Admiral William Penn issued it to his men in place of beer, starting a trend that saw rum established as a part of a British sailor's daily rations for more than 300 years.

By the early 18th century, rum and molasses were Britain's main source of trading income and the most profitable traded commodities in the West Indies. The attempt to stop rum-smuggling along the Atlantic Coast of North America by the imposition of a sugar tax helped to ignite the American Revolutionary War in 1775.

Thinly sliced marinated tuna makes a mouthwateringly delicious starter/appetizer or snack that is surprisingly easy to prepare. Look for the freshest sushi-grade tuna to make this raw dish and serve it as soon as possible after preparation; although the lime or lemon helps to keep it fresh, it rapidly loses its colour if left sitting. Salted capers and anchovy paste add piquancy to the dressing. Caper berries are simply well-developed capers; slightly larger and a little sweeter, they are often sold with the stalks left on.

Tuna carpaccio with capers

500 g/1 lb. fresh tuna loin, sliced into 4 or 6 pieces (ideally by the fishmonger)

8 tablespoons extra virgin olive oil

8 limes or 4 lemons

75 g/8 tablespoons salted capers, rinsed and chopped

1 teaspoon anchovy paste

freshly ground black pepper

fresh nasturtium leaves, caper leaves or rocket/arugula (optional) and 12 caper berries, to garnish

Crusty bread, to serve

Serves 4

Ensure that the tuna is chilled, then place each piece between 2 sheets of greaseproof paper/wax paper. Using a rolling pin, roll and flatten each piece until it's the size of a dinner plate.

Pour a tablespoon of the olive oil onto each of 4 dinner plates, then tilt them so that the oil covers the whole surface.

Gently transfer each slice of tuna to an oiled plate (inverting it is the easiest method). Squeeze 2 of the limes or 1 of the lemons and brush the juice all over the fish. Let stand while the dressing is made: about 5 minutes, no longer.

Put the remaining oil, the juice of 4 more limes or 2 more lemons, the capers and anchovy paste into a food processor. Pulse in brief bursts until chopped, not puréed. Pour into a serving bowl.

Grind some black pepper over the tuna. Cut the remaining limes in half or lemon into wedges and use to garnish the plates, along with the leaves (if using) and the caper berries. Drizzle a circle of dressing over each plate.

Serve without delay, offering crusty bread as an accompaniment.

CASUAL COASTAL

ABOVE Items intended purely for display are seldom seen in this unusual coastal home, but the few exceptions to the rule make an unmistakable reference to their location, such as this simple white bowl overflowing with gastropod shells.

ABOVE Old-fashioned metal hooks look at home in rustic kitchens and provide the means to store cooking utensils while keeping them on show. Painting the metal beam and hook fittings in a washed-out grey colour enhances the seaside feel.

would these be better for the shape of the house

Railway carriage revival

When fashion designer Kate Barton discovered The Dodo in 2002, she and her family didn't like the name of the house at all. They tried hard to think of something that would seem more appropriate for a seaside home, but somehow the name Dodo stuck, and now they have grown rather fond of it. No one knows exactly where the name came from – in the same way that no one knows who created this astonishing house in the first place.

The Dodo overlooks the beach at the Sussex resort of West Wittering – part of a designated Area of Outstanding Natural Beauty embracing the creeks, inlets and tidal flats of Chichester Harbour on England's South Coast. The shoreline features sand dunes, marram grass and tamarisk, and a long line of colourful beach huts.

The story goes that in the 1930s, when a local railway/railroad line was taken out of service,

someone had the inspired idea of installing a couple of defunct railway carriages/railroad cars at right angles to the sea, and parallel to each other, and building a roof over the top of them. 'If you walk along the beach you will see similar houses made from railway carriages, though you often can't tell,' says Kate. 'One of them is a traditional wooden structure that could easily be mistaken for a clapboard cottage in Cape Cod.'

ABOVE After living at The Dodo for two years, Kate and her husband built a wooden porch with a large skylight, giving direct access from the back of the house to the beach. There are two doors in the porch, one opening into the main house and the other into a spare bedroom.

OPPOSITE A wood-burning stove is the focal point of the living space. The pared-back look is enlivened by a trio of wooden seabirds displayed on a high shelf and a scattering of Lloyd Loom armchairs.

OPPOSITE The two old railway carriages/railroad cars, which contain the bedrooms and bathrooms, are linked by an open-plan living space. At the front of the house is a raised dining area with a seagrass carpet. This space is rarely used because, whenever possible, Kate and her family prefer to eat their meals outside on the sundeck. The sofa on the lower level has been covered in indigo Singapore linen from Olicana textiles.

In fact, the practice of turning redundant railway carriages into homes is much more common than might be imagined around the coast of England and Wales, with intriguing examples to be found everywhere from Cornwall to Yorkshire. The generous width of a railway carriage and its abundance of glass can be exploited with relative ease to create beautiful, light-filled modern living spaces.

'When we bought the house, it was very basic, even though another family had lived there for some time,' says Kate. 'There was a small Formica kitchen and one tiny bathroom. Everything was covered in brown gloss paint.'

As the walls were painstakingly stripped and repainted, original details were uncovered, from tongue-and-groove panelling to the friezes on the ceiling. Carpets were removed and the floorboards were repaired, sanded and painted white. Bathrooms and four bedrooms are located in the two former carriages, which are linked by a large, open-plan living space heated by a wood-burning stove.

There is a raised dining area with a seagrass carpet, but the family spend most mealtimes on The Dodo's wide deck enjoying the views of the sea. 'We always eat in the open air, unless the wind is strong enough to blow away the salad leaves,' says Kate.

ABOVE LEFT This sturdy indoor bench, painted greyish purple, is notable for its rough edges and its curvy outline, which complements the rounded edges of the carriage windows.

ABOVE RIGHT Time-worn wooden tables suit the informality of coastal dining spaces. An old-fashioned cutlery/flatware tray and a set of white-painted upright chairs complete this serene interior scene.

OPPOSITE From the curved ceiling with its circular moulding to the row of narrow windows with rounded corners, many elements of the former railway carriage are still in evidence. Muslin curtains soften the hard lines of the metal four-poster, while blue-and-white striped bed linen injects vitality into an otherwise tonal scheme.

THIS PAGE Simple floral displays, such as this single allium stem in a slim vase, create striking focal points in an uncluttered interior.

BELOW AND BELOW RIGHT
Stripped wooden boards and tongue-and-groove panelling give an illusion of space in this unusual bathroom. The opaque glass in the door and windows and the heavy door handle are original features of the railway carriage. Decorative interest comes from the rose motif in the curtains, a Shaker peg rail and an antique model yacht.

RIGHT In this refreshingly light-filled bedroom, subtly striped bed linen and simple Roman blinds provide a harmonious and elegant complement to a pair of iron bedsteads. With five bedrooms in the main house and a twin bedroom in the annexe, The Dodo sleeps up to 12 people and is often rented out to large groups of friends. It is also sometimes used as a writers' retreat.

OPPOSITE Throughout the house, geometric patterns in blinds, bed linen and other fabrics are used to reflect the horizontal and vertical lines of the wall panels and floorboards. In this room, the fitted bunk beds and roughly painted wooden floor evoke the atmosphere of a ship's cabin.

ABOVE Kate's greatest triumph was to turn part of the decked area into an outdoor bathroom. The bathtub was picked up at a reclamation yard and there is a hot shower nearby, which Kate prefers for her own use. 'I've had ten small children in that bathtub at once,' she says. 'They absolutely love it.'

OPPOSITE The beach gets very busy during holiday periods, but the house is shielded from passers-by by a wooden groyne. This manmade barrier, built to limit coastal erosion, also screens people on the beach from those at the house.

Kate and her husband Nigel worked to transform The Dodo into a relaxed and relaxing holiday retreat where they and their five children could escape as often as possible from their high-pressure city lives. The result is a chic and practical family space that needs minimal attention, apart from painting the floors once a year.

After the initial stage of the work was complete, there was a two-year pause before the couple decided to build an extension to incorporate a bigger kitchen, a downstairs bathroom and a utility area, as well as an extra bedroom. A wooden porch was erected, giving direct access from the back of the house to the beach.

Later, a former garage across the road was converted into a separate annexe containing a playroom and a guest bedroom. There is a tiny enclosed garden between the two buildings, which makes a secure play area for small children.

Kate and her family used to stay there for six weeks each year, but now that the children are getting older they go less often. Among other things, The Dodo is used as a writers' retreat, where experienced scribblers and beginners gather for workshops and walks, and plenty of time is set aside for writing and relaxation.

ABOVE Accessories for both indoor and outdoor living have been chosen for their muted colours and appealing textures as well as for their usefulness.

Decorating with beach finds

Beachcombing is a pleasure in its own right and it is particularly satisfying to adorn your home with shoreline finds – but make sure that you do not remove anything from the beach illegally or damage the coastal ecology.

When choosing which treasures to put on display, consider texture and tactility as much as visual appeal. Wave-smoothed pebbles, limpets and thinly grooved scallop shells arranged on a shelf or windowsill will tempt you to pick them up and stroke them. By contrast, dried sea sponges and coarse hemp ropes with chunky knots are pleasingly rough to the touch.

Pieces of bleached driftwood, gnarled and contorted into strange shapes, can be smooth or rough, but are often worth treating as works of art, perhaps displayed on a glass shelf or in a vitrine. Tiny pieces of blue and green glass, their edges rubbed smooth by the action of the sea, are amazingly versatile decorative items.

Feathers, starfish and delicate fronds of dried seaweed are ideal for adding form and texture to an interior display. Place a row of starfish along a bathroom or kitchen shelf for an instant nautical feel. Shells come in a huge variety of colours, shapes and sizes and can be used in myriad ways as containers or to create a decorative effect – glued to mirror frames, strung together to make mobiles, piled into large glass jars, or displayed on trays or table tops with dramatic pink corals.

This thick, satisfying, easy-to-make fish soup is the perfect winter warmer. It is a more elaborate version of Cullen skink, the classic Scottish dish often served as a starter/appetizer. Choose natural oak-smoked haddock, which is particularly delicate and delicious.

Smoked haddock chowder

400 g/14 oz. smoked haddock

100 g/7 tablespoons butter

200 ml/¾ cup milk

1 leek, white only, sliced

1 large white onion, diced

1 large potato, peeled and diced

a good pinch of saffron strands

a pinch of ground turmeric

2 bay leaves

750 ml/3 cups vegetable stock

100 g/generous ½ cup white long-grain or basmati rice

200 ml/¾ cup double/heavy cream

grated zest and freshly squeezed juice of 1 lemon

1 bunch of fresh parsley, chopped

freshly ground black pepper

Serves 6

Preheat the oven to 190°C (375°F) Gas 5.

Put the fish in a baking dish, and brush with 15 g/1 tablespoon of the butter, melted. Pour over the milk and cover the dish with a sheet of kitchen foil. Put the dish in the preheated oven and poach the fish for about 15 minutes, until it is just cooked and opaque. Pour off the poaching liquid, reserving it to add to the soup later. Remove the skin, then debone the fish thoroughly by gently running a finger down the surface of the fish – you should feel the sharp little bones as you go – and pulling out the bones with your fingers or tweezers. Flake the fish into generous pieces, checking for any remaining bones as you go, and set aside.

Melt the remaining butter in a large saucepan and add the leek, onion and potato. Soften over a gentle heat for a few minutes, then add the saffron and tumeric. Add the bay leaves and pour over the stock. Add the rice and stir to prevent it from sticking to the bottom. Simmer for about 12 minutes, stirring occasionally.

When the rice is tender, add the flaked fish to the chowder, along with its poaching liquid. Stir gently and add the cream, lemon zest and the lemon juice, to taste. Stir through the parsley, season well with black pepper and serve.

Fire Island hideaway

Fire Island is a beautiful strip of land running parallel with the southern shore of Long Island, from where it is accessible across a narrow channel by boat, ferry or causeway. Living on Fire Island is synonymous with being on the edge of things. At 43 km (27 miles) long and 400 metres (¼ mile) wide at its widest point, it is the largest in a string of barrier islands shielding their larger neighbour from the mighty Atlantic Ocean, which is at its most threatening during the hurricane season from May to November.

LEFT Saltaire is the docking point for a ferry between Long Island and Fire Island. Its tranquil bay has an abundance of moorings for sailing boats and speedboats. No private cars are allowed on Fire Island, but everything is within easy walking or cycling distance.

ABOVE LEFT AND RIGHT On the Atlantic side of Fire Island is a fabulous sandy beach, popular in summer for swimming, fishing and kite-flying. Wooden boardwalks and sandy paths connect the beach with the bay and marina on the other side of the island.

THIS PAGE Little was done by Alex and Andrew Bates to alter their early 20th-century 'Coffey' house. They retained the original floor plan and kept the kitchen as they found it, including the narrow doorless archway that connects the kitchen to the rest of the living area.

cute!

ABOVE LEFT The glossy blue linoleum flooring, which Alex and Andrew inherited from a previous owner of the house, provides a vibrant contrast to the otherwise all-white kitchen.

ABOVE RIGHT A set of decorative platters once used for serving oysters has been carefully inserted into a wall-hung plate rack above a row of 12 upturned glasses. The arrangement creates a dramatic visual display behind the kitchen table.

Alex and Andrew Bates began to visit Fire Island in the early 1990s and were drawn to the small town of Saltaire, where they eventually bought one of the distinctive 'Coffey' houses for which the island is famous. They loved the peace and solitude of the island and its proximity to New York City, their main home, where both had demanding jobs in professional retail and design. 'It is quite close to the city and yet it seems worlds away,' says Alex, who loved being able to give her three young children a regular taste of rural freedom when they were growing up.

The easy two-hour journey from the city makes it possible for the family to come out to Fire Island for short trips and weekends. 'The off-seasons are our favourite times,' says Alex. 'September is best because the summer people

have left and the weather is still incredible, and the water is warmer than August. There is great fishing off the beach.'

Their house in Saltaire was constructed in 1911 by Mike Coffey, an émigré Irishman who became the town's master builder. Coffey was responsible for more than 100 Saltaire houses, the village hall, three churches and an extension to the yacht club. His cedar-shingled, light-filled buildings are particularly admired for their seamless melding of beauty and functionality. One recurrent feature is a triple vertical windowpane pattern in the upper part of the window (referred to locally as an 'eyebrow' window). Many of these houses were demolished in the Great New England Hurricane of 1938, but some survive and remain in use today.

'We've kept our Coffey house true to the original design,' says Alex. Apart from replacing some old tiles with wood panelling, they kept everything just as it was when they bought it, including the blue linoleum kitchen floor. They simply painted everything white and covered the furniture in white slipcovers. There is no pattern to the choice or arrangement of furniture, which consists of a mixture of found pieces and family hand-me-downs.

A private boardwalk, typical of the area, leads to a large enclosed entrance porch that doubles as a comfortable living room. The cedar shingles on the façade of the house are continued into the interior of this room, where they have been stained a rich dark brown, in stark contrast to the glossy white-painted floor, ceiling and window frames.

BELOW The decorative style was kept simple so that the house would be easy to maintain. Most of the furniture is second-hand, and sofas and chairs are covered in washable white slipcovers. White walls and ceilings make the most of the natural light.

RIGHT The traditional fireplace has a brick surround and chimneypiece that have both been painted glossy white, in keeping with the rest of the room. A shell-framed mirror hangs above the mantelpiece, adding a touch of flamboyance.

Alex and Andrew entertain a lot of friends at small cocktail or dinner parties, but their style is to keep things relaxed and spontaneous. 'Everyone pitches in and on most occasions we are outdoors,' says Alex. They have large extended families and have occasionally packed a surprising number of people into this small house, including lots of children on the floor in sleeping bags. 'This is no place for formality!'

A natural disaster occurred in 2012 when Fire Island was hit by Hurricane Sandy and had to be evacuated. In this instance, the main cause of the damage was water rather than wind and 80 per cent of the houses were flooded. 'The water was three to four feet deep overall, and stayed through a few tides before washing back to sea,' explains Alex. Most of the streets on the island were made of raised wooden boardwalks, which were washed away or buckled dramatically. Luckily, all the remaining Coffey houses survived.

Alex and Andrew had to remove every item from their home and take emergency measures to prevent mould damage, but they kept the wooden floors because they liked the naturally occurring 'cupping' of the boards. 'The whole project was like building a

ABOVE AND ABOVE LEFT The front entrance to the house consists of a covered porch with several other rooms leading off it. The cedar shingles used to clad the outside of the house were continued into the porch, where they have been stained dark brown, in contrast to the white-painted floor, ceiling and window frames. Afternoon sun streams through the windows, and ceiling fans rotate to keep the atmosphere cool. The internal porch window looks back into the master bedroom.

house from the inside out,' says Alex. 'We moved a couple of walls to straighten out some original awkward angles, and put in all new electric wiring and heating, a brand new kitchen and a bathroom.'

They designed the new spaces to feel modern but also to remain respectful of the house's original spirit. The only repair that was needed to the outside of the house was the replacement of some cedar shingles. 'The worst part of the whole thing was that we

and our neighbours had all our gardens and trees destroyed. Twenty years of dedicated gardening lost to salt-water damage!'

On a more positive note, Alex celebrates the fact that Fire Island is a paradise for wildlife. Its mixture of forest, dune and marsh habitats offers feeding and nesting opportunities for a wide array of waterbirds, and much of the island's southern coast is a US National Seashore, a designation intended to protect wild spaces.

LEFT Most Saltaire residents have their own small four-wheeled wagons, which are stationed at the ferry wharf for the transport of luggage and supplies around this car-free hamlet. The wagons are individually named for ease of identification.

ABOVE LEFT AND RIGHT Two small bedrooms adjoin the entrance porch. The bunk-bedded room has its own external window, but the window in the master bedroom looks out onto the porch. The white-painted Venetian blinds maximize privacy and offer an easy way to control the light level.

OPPOSITE The entrance porch is lined on two sides by external windows, with the result that the room is flooded with sunshine on fine days. The built-in window seats with their large, plump cushions not only make a comfortable place for relaxation but also provide additional sleeping space for guests.

To the legendary food writer Elizabeth David, an omelette and a glass of wine evoked the ultimate 'primitive and elemental meal'. Indeed, the method of using a fried egg mixture as a wrap for other cooked food is a feature of many cuisines around the world. The lobster omelette is popular on the east coast of the USA, and is especially irresistible when served with a hollandaise sauce infused with truffle oil.

Maine lobster omelette

6 eggs

170 g/6 oz. fresh lobster meat, chopped

2 teaspoons unsalted butter

sea salt and ground black pepper

115 g/4 oz. tomatoes, chopped

1 teaspoon chives, chopped

Truffle-hollandaise sauce

3 egg yolks

2 tablespoons freshly squeezed lemon juice

115 g/1 stick cold, unsalted butter cut into pieces

¼ teaspoon sea salt

a pinch of freshly ground black pepper

a pinch of paprika

a drizzle of truffle oil

1 chive, chopped, to garnish

Serves 2

To make the truffle-hollandaise sauce, whisk the egg yolks, 60 ml/¼ cup water and lemon juice in a small saucepan until blended. Cook over a very low heat, stirring constantly, until the mixture bubbles at the edges. Stir in the butter, a piece at a time, until it has melted and the sauce has thickened. Remove from the heat immediately and stir in the salt, pepper, paprika and truffle oil. Transfer the sauce to a small serving dish and garnish with the chopped chive.

Whisk the eggs together, then separate the mixture into 2 bowls and set aside.

Spread the lobster onto an oven proof dish and place in the preheated oven for 5 minutes.

Over a medium heat, warm a medium to large non-stick frying pan/skillet and add 1 teaspoon of the butter. As the butter melts, season one portion of the eggs with salt and black pepper. Add this egg mixture to the heated frying pan/skillet and stir gently with a spatula.

Just as the eggs start to set, add half the chopped lobster, half the tomatoes and half the chives to the eggs and stir gently. Stop stirring and allow them to firm for 1–2 minutes. Fold the omelette and slide it out onto a warm plate. Place the plate in the oven to keep the omelette warm. Repeat the same process for the second omelette, then serve both with the truffle-hollandaise sauce.

THIS PAGE Naja Lauf's house at Bellevue has a relaxed, airy feel and gives magnificent views across the Øresund strait and the nearby countryside. Meals are often eaten on the sea-facing terrace, where the simple deck furniture has been painted white to match the horizontal wooden boards lining the space.

La vie est Belle

'We like to live with air and light all around us,' says Naja Lauf, a clothes designer, 'so we set about making a really simple interior that combines calming natural colours with an abundance of white.' The home that Naja has created with her husband John-Allan Holm overlooks fashionable Bellevue Beach in Klampenborg, about 20 minutes' drive from central Copenhagen. As beach inspector for north Copenhagen, John-Allan could hardly have an easier journey to work.

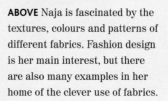

ABOVE Naja is fascinated by the textures, colours and patterns of different fabrics. Fashion design is her main interest, but there are also many examples in her home of the clever use of fabrics.

ABOVE The terrace overlooking the sea is lined by window boxes, where various plants are grown through the year. This is an ideal place to while away a summer evening and watch the sunset.

The yellow-brick house was built in 1890 for a doctor who used it both as a private home and for his clinical consultations. In 1931 it was remodelled when the whole area was transformed into a public park. At that time, the manager of the beach came to live in the house – and it is still that way today, with John-Allan in residence as the fourth beach manager.

'We moved here in 1991,' explains Naja. 'Our first task was to demolish the wall between the kitchen and the dining room and build a new kitchen.' The house was in such poor condition that they had to go back to basics before decoration could start. Several layers of wallpaper were removed from the remaining walls and the old wooden floorboards were sanded but left slightly roughened to resemble the deck of a ship. The floors were then varnished or painted white.

The house at Bellevue is Naja and John-Allan's main home. It is simply constructed over two floors with a basement and a sea-facing wooden deck that gives

LEFT The chairs and table in the more formal dining space are by the Danish architect and designer Arne Jacobsen, who established very strong links with Bellevue during his lifetime. Naja has a love of design classics but tends to shun ostentatious statement pieces. The light hanging above the table is by Poul Henningsen.

THIS PAGE The unusual wooden cabinet with lots of small doors was retrieved from the beach. It was once used by people going for a swim as a locker for their valuables. On top of the cabinet is a painting by Naja's father, Otto Lauf, and binoculars for observing passing ships and boats.

views over the Øresund strait, the channel that separates Denmark from Sweden. The couple make the most of living so close to the water by taking a swim each morning, even in the depths of winter.

'The area is protected to preserve the original work of Jacobsen,' explains Naja. Since the 1930s, Bellevue has been inextricably connected with the Danish architect and furniture designer Arne Jacobsen, whose blue-striped lifeguard towers, geometric kiosks and other distinctive creations still adorn

OPPOSITE A glass-panelled door and white-painted floorboards help to create a feeling of airiness and light, while pale fabrics and a few carefully selected pieces of furniture enhance the pared-back look. The walls have deliberately been left bare so as to reflect as much light as possible.

the beach and continue to exert an influence on local architecture. Jacobsen's Bellevue Theatre is a leading example of Danish Functionalism and his spectacular Modernist Bellavista housing estate also stands nearby.

The move to Bellevue coincided with Naja's decision to set up her own business in Copenhagen after working for a series of big fashion houses across Europe. Her own-brand collections combine reinvented classics with contemporary essentials that focus on unfussy, comfortable styles and

LEFT Propped up in the corner of the living room is a collection of old fishing rods. 'We only bought them because of their beauty,' says Naja. The cane chairs, from Ikea, are made more inviting by the addition of striped cushions from Day Birger et Mikkelsen.

OPPOSITE, ABOVE LEFT A sense of calm pervades the living room. The sofa is from Arketipo, an Italian company, while the coffee table was skilfully made out of a large piece of elm by John-Allan.

OPPOSITE, ABOVE RIGHT The radiators in the bedroom have been incorporated into the scheme – a design trick that is used elsewhere in the house. Here, the geometrical pattern of this heater is mirrored in the cushions on the bed, while the angular light breaks the rigidity.

OPPOSITE, BELOW The original bathtub and wall tiles were retained in the bathroom, which is Naja's favourite room in the house. An old shaving mirror, the enamel pitcher on the radiator and other retro items enhance the room's traditional feel.

innovative detailing. Naja wears all the clothes she designs and likes to experiment with different shapes and fabrics.

This love of simplicity and clean lines is evident in the interior decoration of the house at Bellevue, which has just two bedrooms. The colour scheme is cool and pared back, and most of the windows have been left undressed to admit maximum light and to give unrestricted views of the Øresund channel. The only room that was kept as it was found is the bathroom, which is unusually large for such an old house and retains its original bathtub and

off-white wall tiles. The other rooms are a dining room, a living room, a utility room and two offices.

'Since the building is next to the beach, we decided to give it a summerhouse feel,' says Naja. 'For us, this is synonymous with a relaxing atmosphere. It also provides an energizing base for our daily lives and we don't have to worry much about it. Living like this makes us feel free.' Unless it is blowing a gale, meals are eaten outside on the terrace above the sea, where eight people can sit down at the table. There is even an outdoor kitchen. 'The weather

here is normally very good, even when it's bad inland,' says Naja, who adds that the terrace is a perfect place to relax on long summer evenings in the light of an old storm lantern. On chillier days, the family use the indoor dining area, where a table and chairs by Arne Jacobsen and a pendant light by Poul Henningsen reflect the couple's love of design classics.

In this corner of the living room there is a wooden cabinet with numerous small doors that provides useful storage. Surprisingly, it came from the beach – an unusual shoreline find. 'It was originally designed as a set of lockers, where visitors could put their valuables while they went for a swim,' explains Naja. 'When it wasn't needed any more, we decided to give it a home.' On top of the cabinet is an assortment of binoculars, used to observe the constant comings and goings of vessels on the busy waterway between Sweden and Denmark.

A feeling of intense calm pervades the living room, whose white walls have been left almost bare to reflect as much light as possible. There are cane chairs from Ikea and striped cushions from Day Birger et Mikkelsen, while the coffee table was made by John-Allan out of a large piece of elm. The large, comfortable sofa comes from the Italian company Arketipo.

Displaying nautical maps and charts

If you are a true sailor – or simply dream about being one – there is no better way to create the illusion of a life afloat than by displaying nautical paraphernalia in your home. You can transform any space into a veritable ship's cabin by framing old maritime maps and charts behind glass and hanging them on walls, or even covering an entire room with a nautically themed wallpaper.

While their main purpose was to alert sailors to navigational hazards, many old ships' documents are also historically revealing. Victorian-era maps of the Thames in London, for example, show a bustling waterway crammed with

warehouses and docks trading in every imaginable commodity – a river at the hub of empire. Ocean charts, by comparison, can transport you to an alien underwater world where extraordinary sea creatures thrive, such as the mile-deep Monterey Canyon off the coast of California.

Electronic navigational charts are gradually taking over from paper charts, but many mariners still carry paper charts for peace of mind. In the past, as well as a knowledge of the stars, sailors also relied on instruments such as sextants, compasses and marine chronometers – all fine items for display in a marine-themed space. Other items associated with a seaborne life that work well in a modern interior include wooden or metal step-ladders, ropes, ship's lanterns, signal flags and fishing nets, while horizontal tongue-and-groove panelling recalls the inside of a boat's hull.

Buy the freshest large or jumbo prawns/shrimp you can find and sauté them while still in their shells. This allows the meat inside to cook without drying out, but take care not to overcook them – remove from the pan as soon as they turn opaque. The accompanying salsa is simple to make and full of warm spice. The chilli/chile and coriander/cilantro accentuates, rather than overpowers, the flavour of the seafood.

Prawns/shrimp with spicy salsa

2 green or red tomatoes

1 tablespoon very finely chopped white onion

1 green chilli/chile

1 small bunch of coriander/ cilantro, finely chopped

¼ teaspoon sea salt

15 g/1 tablespoon butter

6 large raw prawns/shrimp, shells on

5 garlic cloves, very finely chopped

stovetop griddle pan/grill pan (optional)

Serves 2

Put the tomatoes, onion, chilli/chile and 500 ml/2 cups water in a saucepan over a high heat. Cover with a lid and bring to the boil, then turn the heat down to low and simmer for about 5–7 minutes.

Drain, then allow to cool for at least 5 minutes before transferring to a food processor with the coriander/cilantro and half the salt. Whizz for 2 minutes and set aside.

Heat a stovetop griddle pan/grill pan or frying pan/skillet over a medium heat. Put the butter and prawns/shrimp in the pan and cook for 3–4 minutes, or until opaque and cooked through, turning occasionally. Add the garlic and cook for 2 minutes.

Divide the prawns/shrimp between 2 dishes and spoon some of the coriander/ cilantro salsa over them. Serve with the remaining salsa on the side.

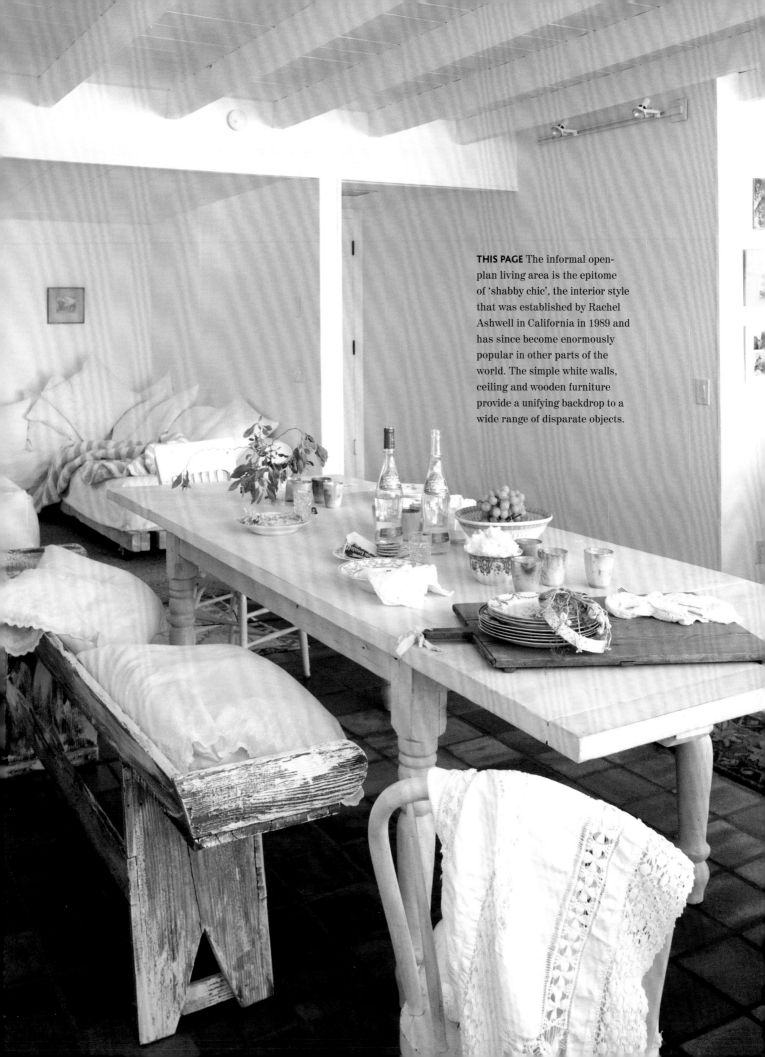

THIS PAGE The informal open-plan living area is the epitome of 'shabby chic', the interior style that was established by Rachel Ashwell in California in 1989 and has since become enormously popular in other parts of the world. The simple white walls, ceiling and wooden furniture provide a unifying backdrop to a wide range of disparate objects.

A beach shack in Malibu

Rachel Ashwell's love affair with Malibu began in 1979, the year she moved from Britain to California, and has only grown more intense with the passing years. Her first experience of living in Malibu dates from the birth of her daughter Lily and son Jake in the 1980s. 'We had a home on the ocean for most of their upbringing, which is a magical playground,' she says. 'It was also the same time that I started my business, Shabby Chic.' The simple beachside home featured here, which Rachel describes as a 'shack', is furnished almost entirely with characterful pieces from her Shabby Chic Couture stores.

ABOVE LEFT Rachel believes that interior style should appeal to all the senses, not just the visual. For that reason, she places great emphasis on music and soft lighting, and includes flowers in her decorative schemes.

ABOVE RIGHT Life at this rustic beach shack in Malibu centres on the broad, glassed-in deck, where family and visitors can congregate to talk and contemplate the ever-changing moods of the ocean. Patterned fabrics and pieces of vintage clothing suspended from a wire by linen pegs add visual interest.

Malibu occupies an extraordinarily beautiful strip of land between the Pacific Ocean and the sheer precipices of the Santa Monica mountains. To many, the town is associated with nothing more than extreme wealth and Hollywood stars, but Rachel Ashwell has always managed to find an unpretentious bolt-hole there where she can experiment with 'shabby chic', the wonderfully successful interior style that she established more than 25 years ago. 'I was drawn to this shack after I'd sold a cottage elsewhere,' says Rachel. 'Even though I didn't intend to live in Malibu full time, I was longing for a little getaway. Malibu homes on the beach can be

expensive, so I had to be realistic about how to achieve my desire within a limited budget.'

Built in the 1950s, the beach house is thought to have originally been a love nest for film stars, but not much is known about its later history. The pressure on building land here means that there are other houses on both sides, so privacy is limited, but all the houses along the beach are orientated towards the ocean, which acts as a natural sound barrier and offers some breathtaking views.

Rachel initially found the beach house rather ugly with a badly organized interior layout, but she really enjoys a challenge of this nature. 'A coat of white paint, pretty candlelight, flowers and some mushy sofas are transformational.'

The original house had consisted of just one bedroom, a bathroom, a living room and a kitchen, but it had grown organically over the years. The central core of the property is a wood-framed deck, which was added after the main

house. It was enclosed with tall glass walls and partially covered by a latticework trellis. An extra bedroom and bathroom were later added at one end of the deck and, more recently, two more bedrooms and one bathroom were built at a lower level, reached by an unusual spiral staircase that also leads down to a small swimming pool.

Although Rachel calls the layout 'disjointed' and 'a hodgepodge', she likes the fact that it provides a lot of privacy, which is ideal when the house is full of guests. Residents and visitors spend most of the time on the deck, which is furnished with assorted chairs and tables, and from where there is direct access to the beach.'

When Rachel and her family arrived, the colour palette of the interior was predominantly beige, 'my most hated colour'. She immediately set about painting the walls, ceilings and woodwork white and covering the floors with vintage rugs. 'To distract from the time-worn vibe and the beige, I took my inspiration from Ibiza and the

OPPOSITE, ABOVE Rachel has created what she describes as 'snoozing spaces' in every available corner and filled them with daybeds and sectional sofas from her stores. Throughout the house, except for a few voile panels, there are no curtains to obstruct the wonderful views.

LEFT A utilitarian pendant light is given a dramatic flourish by the addition of an arrangement of artificial flowers and leaves sprayed with silver leaf.

BELOW LEFT The predominance of white is evident in every room in the house. 'I used to think that white was non-committal and boring,' says Rachel, 'but I have learned that white is a neutral wow, and one that can be a brave statement.'

BELOW RIGHT The rooms are given individuality and character by the inclusion of vintage fabrics, furnishings and display items such as books, table lamps and flower vases.

141

THIS PAGE Rachel always takes great care not to introduce clutter into her bedrooms. 'I think bedrooms should be revered as sanctuaries, the places where we have our first and last thoughts of the day, and should therefore have only beautiful bare necessities.'

Greek islands, says Rachel. 'My palette was white and aqua blue.
All the soft furnishings were white – sofas, bedding and so on.
I layered throws and pillows of blues, aqua stripes and voiles.'
Rachel now spends most of her time at her main house in
Brentwood, Los Angeles, about 32km/20 miles from Malibu,
but she still escapes to the beach whenever she can.

To Rachel, one of the wonderful things about a second home,
especially one on the beach, is that it feels completely acceptable,
even desirable, to fill it with second-hand furnishings and other
items – so any old linens and towels, for example, from a former
existence that still have life in them are given a new purpose
at her beach house. 'I like to mix vintage elements into my
furnishings by way of fabrics or furniture to give individuality
and soul to a room,' she says.

Rachel argues that it is crucial to analyse the function of a
room and take account of the lifestyle of its inhabitants, before
embarking on a decorative makeover. Her mantra in decoration
is that every single element she chooses must combine beauty,
comfort and function. 'All my decisions are filtered through that
philosophy,' says Rachel. 'Also, although I welcome hodgepodge
and mismatch, I must have some kind of order in the chaos, so
I try to stick with a unifying palette, which is various shades of
white, blues, pinks and grey, from pastel to smoky.'

Candlelight and a few vintage lights dotted through an interior
always add hints of romance. Rachel believes that a home should
engage all the senses to feel whole, and for that reason she gives
a great deal of attention to soft lighting and music, flowers and
comfort. 'My aesthetic is romantic and nourishing, and has soul.
Less is more with mindful and meaningful choices.'

ABOVE RIGHT Virtually every
item used to furnish the Malibu
beach shack is available at the
Shabby Chic Couture stores, and
all these items were originally
handpicked by Rachel, including
antique pieces, upholstery for
custom-made sofas and artisan-
crafted chandeliers.

RIGHT As well as being a
showcase for Rachel's range of
popular homewares, the house
contains many personal objects,
from family portaits to pinboards
and vintage dresses. The fabrics
and pieces of clothing hung up
in several rooms are part of
the decorative scheme.

Fish fingers may seem an unlikely filling for a sandwich, but the ensemble works deliciously well in this recipe. Lager is added to the batter to create a richer flavour.

Posh fish finger sandwich and tartare sauce

2 skinned and pin-boned fillets of cod or haddock

sunflower or vegetable oil, for frying

sea salt

French country bread, to serve

butter, for spreading

handful of cos/romaine lettuce leaves, cut into strips, to serve

hand-cut fries, to serve

Beer batter

200 g/1½ cups plain/all-purpose flour

2 teaspoons sea salt

2 x 330 ml/12 fl. oz. bottles of lager

Homemade tartare sauce

225 g/1 cup mayonnaise

80 g/½ cup dill pickles/gherkins

1 teaspoon capers, chopped

2 teaspoons Dijon mustard

2 teaspoons chopped shallots

2 tablespoons spring onions/scallions, chopped

2 teaspoons lemon juice

Tabasco sauce, to taste

sea salt and freshly ground black pepper

Makes 2

Prepare your fish for battering. If the fish isn't already skinned and boned, do so. Slice the fish into a number of finger-sized strips.

For the batter, whisk the flour, salt and lager in a bowl until combined.

Fill a large frying pan/skillet with about 2.5 cm/1 in. oil over a high heat, but don't leave this unattended. When the oil is bubbling steadily, it's ready to go. Dip the fish fingers in the batter, remove any excess and then lower carefully into the oil using tongs if necessary. Fry for about 4 minutes on each side over a moderate heat until golden and crispy.

Carefully remove the fish fingers from the oil and drain well on paper towels. Season with sea salt.

While the fish fingers are frying, mix all the ingredients for the tartare sauce together in a mixing bowl.

Cut the French country bread into thick slices. Lay one down and butter it before spreading a couple of tablespoons of tartare sauce on top. Place 3 fish fingers on top, then a few strips of lettuce, before placing a second slice of bread on top. Serve with hand-cut fries.

RUSTIC COASTAL

THIS PAGE Occupying centre stage in the dining room is an amazing medieval table. Made from one piece of oak, it measures about 3 metres (10 feet) in length. The table came from the house of Marta's late father, an architect, who was given it by a client whose estate he was renovating.

Remote and romantic

When you walk out onto the seashore at Jury's Gap and take in the panoramic view, you can be forgiven for thinking that you are in the middle of nowhere. The wild beach stretches for 6.5 km (4 miles) in each direction, and even during the summer season it is often deserted. Yet Jury's Gap is located near the tip of southeast England in one of the most densely populated regions of the country. Marta Nowicka, an interior architect, fell in love with an old coastguard cottage here in 2009 after many years of searching for her ideal seaside home.

TOP LEFT Many of the second-hand pieces in the former coastguard cottage have an intriguing story attached to them. This delicately wrought metal shelf, for example, had an earlier life in a French *boulangerie*, where freshly baked loaves were left on top to cool.

ABOVE LEFT The utilitarian style of a couple of old school chairs is ideally suited to the relaxed ambience of the cottage, where there is not much room to spare. When not in use, they can be neatly stacked in an alcove.

ABOVE RIGHT An airy, spacious feel was created in the kitchen by the removal of a suspended ceiling, which dated from the 1960s. Marta then installed an industrial-style kitchen with a functional design and high-quality, stainless-steel appliances.

THIS PAGE Quite a lot of the furniture came from Marta's late father's house, including the outsize clock in the living room. Other pieces were picked up in the local towns of New Romney and Rye, known for their antiques shops. Fireplaces that had been put in during the 1950s were removed, but areas of brickwork on the chimney breasts have been left bare.

The waters along this part of the English coast have long been notorious for shipwrecks – which explains the presence of the isolated row of former coastguard cottages, dating from late Victorian times, that Marta Nowicka discovered at Jury's Gap in 2009. She bought a five-bedroom cottage at the end of the terrace, which had been left empty for more than three years and badly vandalized. 'There was graffitti everywhere,' she says. 'The bathrooms had been smashed up and the radiators pulled off the walls.'

Although Marta found the house eerie at first, she saw its potential. The rooms were small and cosy with exceptionally thick walls, offering vital protection in winter against sea gales, and the old panelling, dado rails and built-in cupboards were still intact. 'It looked really poetic,' she says.

THIS PAGE Every window offers an exhilarating seascape or a view of the nearby countryside. The beach stretches east towards the shingle promontory of Dungeness and west towards Camber Sands and the ancient town of Rye. Behind the house is a wildlife haven that sometimes doubles as a military firing range.

Rustic Coastal

LEFT These wonderful old paint-flaked shutters convey a distinct flavour of France. Marta has consciously tried to give the house a French feel, liking to recall that the nearby town of Rye was one of the ancient Cinque Ports, a league of military and trading towns along England's southeast coast that maintained strong links with France.

BELOW LEFT A quilt with coloured tassels and a vibrant pillowslip add warmth and cosiness to a child's bedroom. The under-bed drawers provide invaluable extra storage.

OPPOSITE Marta extended the living space upwards into the attic, converting the otherwise redundant roof space into a secluded guest bedroom with far-reaching views over Camber Sands. Continuing the nautical theme, the rafters are clad in white-painted tongue-and-groove panelling reminiscent of the interior of a boat.

BELOW RIGHT One of the most imaginative interior features of the coastguard cottage is a nautical-style wooden ladder built into a corner of the first-floor landing, which leads up to the attic bedroom.

There was even a gun room in the cottage, where the coastguards would have stored the weapons needed to scare off looters after shipwrecks. Marta, who runs an interior architecture business in London, describes the style of the terrace as 'standard vernacular coastguard design'.

A lover of solitude, Marta was particularly drawn to the remote and romantic nature of the location, which is halfway between the popular resort of Camber Sands and the vast shingle promontory of Dungeness. Behind the house is a wildlife haven that doubles as a military range; when firing practice is not in progress, it is a wonderful place to explore.

Dungeness is a desolate landscape, peppered by wooden shacks, gravel pits, lighthouses and a power station, but it is also the site of a National Nature Reserve with a rich and diverse wildlife,

ABOVE The tiny master bedroom is full of visual interest. Set off by a simple background of white paint and crisp white linens, the exquisite old-gold colour of the plaster wall – replicated in the vase on the mantelpiece – creates a real sense of opulence. The intricate abstract painting complements the decorative detail on the original fireplace.

OPPOSITE Most of the long wall in the bathroom is taken up by a disproportionately large window, while the luxuriously deep tub has been scaled down in size in order to fit into the space.

including a multitude of rare plants and insects. The pioneering garden created by the film director Derek Jarman at his Dungeness home was the inspiration for Marta's large pebbled garden at Jury's Gap, which is ornamented with flotsam and jetsam and driftwood containers.

As restoration of the coastguard cottage got under way, fireplaces that had been put in during the 1950s were removed and floorboards throughout the house were lightly sanded and oiled. The interior walls were stripped back to the original plaster, with some being left unadorned and others painted white.

Areas of brickwork on the chimney breasts were also deliberately left bare. The aim was to allow the imperfections and natural elements of the building to take centre stage.

The 1960s kitchen that Marta found when she moved into the cottage was utterly transformed by the removal of a suspended ceiling. The new

height gave the room an airy, spacious feeling. Marta then installed an industrial-style kitchen with a functional design and high-quality, stainless-steel appliances. 'I needed a decent fridge and oven to cater for all the friends who come to stay,' she explains. During the first summer in which the house was habitable, she entertained 58 guests in a three-month period. Marta still enjoys having visitors, but she also likes to spend time there on her own or in the company of her son, Lucas.

One of the most intriguing elements of the house is a narrow, nautical-style wooden ladder built into a corner of the first-floor landing, which leads up to an attic bedroom with far-reaching views over Camber Sands towards the town of Rye. Continuing the nautical theme, the rafters of the roof space are covered in white-painted tongue-and-groove panelling that is strongly reminiscent of the interior of a boat.

One of the myriad culinary delights of Asturias in northern Spain is *fabada*, a bean stew containing chorizo, morcilla (black pudding) and ham. The most important ingredient is *fabes asturianas*, the prized white beans grown in the region, which are used in many different recipes. This example, known locally as *fabes con almejas*, introduces a taste of the sea to what originated as a wholesome, warming peasant dish. It takes advantage of the abundance of seafood harvested on the Costa Verde.

White beans with clams

30 saffron strands

500 g/2¾ cups dried white beans, such as *fabes asturianas*, cannellini or butter/lima beans, soaked in cold water overnight and drained

1 onion, chopped

3 garlic cloves, chopped

1 carrot, peeled and chopped

1 small bunch of fresh flat-leaf parsley, tied together with string

2 fresh or dried bay leaves

3 tablespoons olive oil

24 live clams, soaked in salt water for a few hours

2 tablespoons white wine

1 tablespoon sweet paprika or pimentón (optional)

salt and freshly ground black pepper

crusty bread, to serve

Serves 4–6

Crumble the saffron into a small bowl and pour 1 tablespoon hot water over it, then leave to infuse while you prepare the rest of the ingredients.

Place the beans, onion, garlic, carrot, parsley, bay leaves and olive oil in a large saucepan, then add enough water to cover everything and bring to the boil. After boiling briskly for 10 minutes, turn the heat down very low, cover the pan and cook for 1½–3 hours, until the beans are soft. During this time, shake the pan every so often, but don't stir the contents or the beans will break up. If necessary, add extra hot water just to cover the beans, but taking care not to drown them.

Towards the end of the cooking time, drain the clams and place in a separate saucepan with the white wine and cook over a medium heat, with the lid on, until all the clams have opened. This will only take a few minutes – lift the lid to inspect every minute or so and take off the heat as soon as they have all opened. Discard any that refuse to open.

Add the saffron and its golden liquid to the pan of beans and remove the bunch of parsley and the bay leaves. Stir in the sweet paprika or pimentón (if using). Using tongs, transfer the clams to the pan of beans, then strain the cooking liquid into the pan, using a fine sieve/strainer or muslin/cheesecloth to remove any grit.

Shake the pan gently from side to side to amalgamate all the juices without breaking up the beans. Simmer everything together gently for a few minutes to blend the flavours. Add salt and black pepper to taste.

Spoon the beans into shallow soup bowls, place 4–6 clams on each and serve with crusty bread, and a glass of dry cider, as they do in Asturias.

Living with blue and white

From the palest aquamarine to the deepest indigo, the spectrum of blues offers endless possibilities for coastal-style decoration. When mixed with creamy white or oyster grey in stripes and other geometric patterns, the blue cornucopia becomes even richer. Blue-and-white patterns incorporating nautical motifs such as boats, seagulls and beach scenes are another variation on the theme. If you live by the ocean, there is no better way to bring the outside in than through the marriage of blue and white.

Blue is the colour we think of at the start of each day when we glance at the morning sky. In general, the bluer the sky, the more cheerful we feel.

Even the powdery grey-blues associated with Scandinavia and other northern latitudes can lift the spirits and provide a perfect light for artists, injecting interiors with sophisticated calm. By contrast, the confident, saturated Caribbean blues recall the intensity of a tropical sea fringed with white sand under the glare of the midday sun.

Blue is a very dominant colour that can make other colours look dirty or dull, which may be why the mixture of warm clear blues with fresh chalky whites is perennially popular. White on its own can make a room seem lighter, airier and more invigorating, but the addition of blue, even in the form of ornaments, textiles or simple decorative details, will make a white scheme less sterile.

50 ml/¼ cup extra virgin olive oil

4 garlic cloves, chopped

2 onions, sliced

6 tomatoes, chopped

1 large fresh bouquet garni: orange zest, parsley, thyme, celery and fennel, tied together

450 g/1 lb. small rockfish or the carcasses (without gills) of cod, whiting, etc.

200 ml/¾ cup dry white wine

2 pinches of saffron strands

1 teaspoon sea salt flakes

½ teaspoon chilli flakes/dried hot red pepper flakes (optional)

Fish

1 cleaned scorpion fish or red gurnard, cut into 2-cm/¾-in. slices

1 x 12-cm/5-in. piece monkfish fillet, cut into 2-cm/¾-in. slices

1 x 12-cm/5-in. piece John Dory or bream fillet, cut into 2-cm/¾-in. slices

1 x 12-cm/5-in. piece red snapper, cut into 2-cm/¾-in. slices

4 cleaned small red mullet or 1 large, cut into 2-cm/¾-in. slices

2 tablespoons pastis (optional)

other additions, such as tiny crabs (optional)

Rouille

1 large red (bell) pepper

4 garlic cloves, peeled

1 medium red chilli/chile, deseeded and roughly chopped

½ teaspoon smoked paprika (hot or mild, as preferred)

180 ml/¾ cup extra virgin olive oil

2 tablespoons fresh white breadcrumbs

sea salt and freshly ground black pepper

Croûtes

1 baguette/French stick

olive oil, for brushing

To serve

Rouille (see recipe)

24 croûtes (see recipe)

100 g/scant 1 cup Gruyère cheese, grated

Serves 4–6

Bouillabaisse originated in Marseilles, where it was made by fishermen using the bony rockfish that they couldn't sell in the markets. As its popularity spread to other parts of France, all sorts of additions were made, including mussels and lobster. Disregarding the many disputes about the correct ingredients, the American chef Julia Child insisted that the 'telling' flavour of the dish depended on two things: 'the Provençal soup base – garlic, onions, tomatoes, olive oil, fennel, saffron, thyme, bay and usually a bit of dried orange peel; and, of course, the fish – lean (non-oily), firm-fleshed, soft-fleshed, gelatinous – and shellfish.'

Classic bouillabaisse

First make the rouille. Place the red (bell) pepper under a hot grill/broiler and cook for 5 minutes on both sides, so that it softens and the skin is slightly charred. Remove the pepper from the grill/broiler and peel the skin with a small knife. Halve the pepper, remove the seeds and roughly chop the flesh.

Place the garlic, chilli/chile, red (bell) pepper and smoked paprika in a food processor or blender and puree to a smooth paste. With the motor running, gradually pour in the olive oil until well combined. Finally, blend in the breadcrumbs. Season the rouille to taste and set aside until ready to serve the bouillabaisse.

Next make the croutes. Preheat the oven to 180°C (350°F) Gas 4. Slice the baguette/French stick into slices about 1 cm/½ inch thick. Arrange them on a baking sheet. Brush lightly on both sides with olive oil. Bake in the preheated oven for 3–4 minutes until lightly browned and crisp.

To make the bouillabaisse, heat the oil in a heavy-based saucepan or flameproof casserole and sauté the garlic and onions over a high heat for 2 minutes. Add the tomatoes, bouquet garni and the rockfish. Cook hard for 3 more minutes. Pour in 1.5 litres/quarts cold water and the wine, and bring back to the boil. Skim off any scum, then boil hard for 8–10 minutes, pressing down on the fish to extract all their flavours.

Meanwhile, using a pestle and mortar, pound together the saffron, salt and chilli flakes/dried hot red pepper flakes (if using). Stir half the mixture into the soup, turn off the heat and let stand for 5 minutes more.

Ladle and/or pour the pan contents into a colander or large sieve/strainer set over a bowl. Press down hard to extract all the juices and flavours but do not mash. Discard these solids, but reserve the bouquet garni.

Return the soup to its original saucepan. Add the 5 fish types in the order listed in the ingredients, leaving the more delicate ones until last: these will sit on top.

Sprinkle over the remaining saffron mixture and add the reserved bouquet garni. Bring the pan contents to a gentle boil and cook for 2 minutes. Reduce the heat to a lively simmer, then part-cover and cook for 5–8 minutes more, or until all the fish is tender and very hot. Taste the liquid and adjust the seasoning, if necessary; it should be a spicy reddish broth.

Add several croûtes, each with a spoonful of rouille on top, and a sprinkle of Gruyère to the pan. To serve the broth, ladle it into individual dishes. Serve the fish after the broth, offering any remaining croûtes, rouille and cheese with it.

The light fantastic

Elena Colombo's simple beachside home at Greenport, on the north fork of Long Island, used to be several hundred yards further inland than it is today. Along with 30 similar homes, built more than a century ago to house employees of the Sage Brick Co., it was moved nearer to the shore after the Great Hurricane of 1938. Before the hurricane, red Sage bricks had been manufactured in their hundreds of millions to construct buildings all over the United States, including some iconic structures in Manhattan. But when floods inundated the clay pits on which brick production depended, the company was forced to close.

ABOVE Elena was drawn to this relaxing corner of Long Island by the marvellous quality of the light, which acts as a magnet to photographers and artists. The simplicity of her home has led some to describe it as a 'shack'.

ABOVE A circular mirror above a high stool adds a new dimension to the food preparation area.

LEFT The original butler's sink continues to perform a useful service in an old-fashioned kitchen that is enlivened by apple-green walls and an informal display of glass jars, propped pictures, vases and biscuit/cookie moulds.

OPPOSITE In common with every other room in the house, the kitchen, which doubles as a dining space, is furnished with pieces from junk shops and the popular local 'dump' – a place where you can leave or take away whatever you like. Elena's success in finding treasures on almost every visit has led her to believe that she is blessed with 'dump luck'.

The resourceful owner of the brick works moved his employees' cottages to the shore of Peconic Bay and rented them out for many years as summer cabins. The works itself was replaced by a marina, but long afterwards bricks continued to be washed up on the shore. 'We used them to make terraces and walkways – so, in theory, the brick works are still with us,' says Elena, who has a deep and abiding love of the place.

Elena discovered the house at Greenport in 1994 and then came back year after year. In 2000 she was part of a co-operative buyout, which had been hurriedly put together to prevent the development of the site as a luxury resort. 'We were a really disparate group and it was a big challenge to make the co-op arrangement work,' she recalls, 'None of us realized how hard it would be to get agreement on the multitude of decisions we had to make,'

Some 36 hectares (90 acres) of land around the cottages, as well as most of the cottages themselves, are commonly owned. 'We have a community garden and a clubhouse where we congregate for fun and games, as well as listening to popular bands,' says Elena. The owners of ten or so of the houses often organize communal waterside dinners on 4 July and other official holidays, and old and young enjoy themselves equally. 'The place is brilliant for kids because they can be outside all day and do physical activities, such as playing soccer, or simply roam free.'

Restricted by planning laws that, among other things, allowed only three per cent expansion on the building's footprint, Elena modernized her house in gradual stages. Her first priority was to install a cedar-shingle roof, but six layers of asphalt had to be removed before work could begin. The builders discovered that the old roofing boards were still in place, so the new roof was laid in accordance with the original pattern.

The cottage now has electrical heating and an open fireplace, which means that Elena can stay there in winter if she wants to, but she also has responsibility for a family home in Pennsylvania, as well as a base in New York City, so she tends not to visit Long Island much during the colder months. Apart from a handful of hardy people who live there all year round, Greenport is mostly a summer community.

ABOVE LEFT Flowery cushion covers combined with a colourful striped blanket add warmth and vibrancy to the small sun room at the back of the house.

ABOVE RIGHT Soon after the co-operative buyout, the house was given a new cedar-shingle roof, but several layers of asphalt had to be removed before re-roofing could begin. Luckily, most of the old roofing boards were still in place, so the shingles could be laid in the original pattern.

OPPOSITE Elena prides herself on using found objects to decorate her seaside home. Some are picked up on the beach, others come from local thrift stores as well as the community swap centre. The back porch is a fine example of the powerful effect that can be achieved by the clever display of simple objects such as old candlesticks and tools.

ABOVE A set of mismatched bone-handled knives, an assortment of multicoloured dinner plates and some retro table napkins make the perfect ensemble for enjoying an alfresco meal. Like many other pieces in Elena's house, these items were bought secondhand from local thrift stores.

ABOVE Elena is a sculptor and has always been attracted by the shapes and textures of natural objects associated with the seashore, such as shells, stones and driftwood. She uses metal, stone, wood and bone found on or near the property to create original pieces of art and then displays them around her home.

The cottages vary in size. Three of them are very large, each with a floor area of about 110 square metres (1,200 square feet), while the rest have only one or two rooms and total floor areas of about 28 square metres (300 square feet). Elena's cottage is somewhere in the middle and isas simply decorated as all the rest.

Elena resolved to spend no more than $100 on any single item that she bought for her home. She picks up all sorts of things, including books, from junk shops and recycling centres. There is a local dump where people can drop off whatever they want and take whatever they want. 'I am always finding real treasures there, such as beautiful old table lamps,' says Elena. 'In fact, I'm convinced that I am blessed with what I call "dump luck".'

During the first half of the 20th century, Greenport was famed as a centre of the lucrative oyster industry and there were once as many as 14 oyster-processing companies here. Although this business has long since declined, locally caught fish remain abundant here, as Elena explains. 'There's flounder and bluefish to be had and, in the bay, bass and blowfish – what we call chicken of the sea. There are mussels and clams and lobster out near the sound.'

One of the exceptional qualities of the area is its wonderful coastal light, making it particularly appealing to photographers and artists. 'The light out here takes my breath away. It is an essential feature of the place,' says Elena. 'We live outside as much as inside, and in midsummer it stays light late into the evening.'

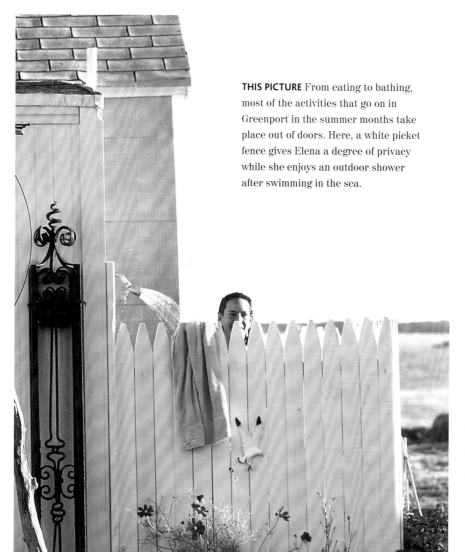

THIS PICTURE From eating to bathing, most of the activities that go on in Greenport in the summer months take place out of doors. Here, a white picket fence gives Elena a degree of privacy while she enjoys an outdoor shower after swimming in the sea.

OPPOSITE Blues, greens and sandy yellows predominate in the interior colour schemes, providing constant reminders of the house's location, while occasional shots of red and orange add touches of drama.

beautiful
wall
color

But the weather is not quite as reliable and can change in an instant. 'We have everything from still, hot, humid days to driving hail and hurricanes.'

Elena is a sculptor and architectural designer who works in steel, bronze, stone, concrete and bone. She runs a business in Brooklyn making outdoor fire features specially designed for their location. 'I am ever inspired by the elemental nature of fire, and the primal need we have for it,' she says. 'Fire serves both our need for beauty and our instinct to gather around a warm lighted place.'

ABOVE LEFT Resembling a giant galvanized bucket, the indoor tub fits neatly into the tiny bathroom, which is enlivened with bright beach towels and primitive pictures. Most of the time, when the weather is good, Elena and her guests prefer to take a shower in the open air.

LEFT A guest bedroom has been decorated with sea-green walls, and, to reinforce the air of informality, an old mirror has been propped between the beds. Apart from the bed linen, most items in the room have come from junk shops, but the fan quilt was bought new from a vintage fabric store.

ABOVE RIGHT A glass-fronted kitchen cupboard, once used for displaying plates and glasses, has found a new life as a place to store clothes and linens.

THIS PAGE To make the most of the natural light that floods this bedroom, original tongue-and-groove walls are painted a soft white, as is the plain iron bedstead. The few decorative items – a straw hat, a single picture, a glass lamp – each makes a strong individual statement.

GOOD-NIGHT

The classic Italian pasta dish known as *spaghetti con frutti di mare* is a celebration of food from the sea. Italy has a wonderful variety of seafood pastas, from *spaghetti vongole*, which originated in Naples, to spaghetti and sea urchins in Puglia, to the Venetian black spaghetti with cuttlefish. In all cases, to obtain perfect results, the seafood used in making the dish must be supremely fresh.

Spaghetti with 'fruits of the sea'

3 tablespoons olive oil

2 garlic cloves, roughly chopped

1 onion, finely chopped

2 fresh or dried bay leaves

sea salt

300 g/2 cups cherry tomatoes

½ teaspoon sugar

125 ml/½ cup sweet white wine

500 g/1 lb. live mussels

16 medium raw prawns/shrimp, peeled and deveined

12 shelled and cleaned scallops

300 g/10 oz. monkfish fillet, cut into 3-cm/1¼-in. pieces

400 g/14 oz. dried spaghetti

freshly ground black pepper

Serves 4

Heat the oil in a large frying pan set over a high heat. Add the garlic, onion, bay leaves and a pinch of salt. Cook for 5 minutes, stirring often. Add the tomatoes, sugar and wine. Bring the mixture to the boil for 2–3 minutes, until the tomatoes have softened. Add 250 ml/1 cup water to the pan and boil for 5 minutes, gently pressing on the tomatoes so that they split. Remove the pan from the heat.

Meanwhile, scrub the mussels well, knock off any barnacles and pull off the beards. Discard any broken mussels and any that won't close when they are tapped on the work surface. Drain in a colander and set aside until needed.

Bring a large saucepan of water to the boil. Add the prawns/shrimp, scallops and monkfish and poach in the water for 2 minutes. Remove with a slotted spoon and add to the tomato sauce.

Return the water to the boil. Add the spaghetti and cook for 10–12 minutes, until tender yet still firm to the bite. Drain well.

Bring the tomato sauce back to high heat. Add the mussels, cover and cook for 4–5 minutes, until the mussels open. Discard any that don't open. Add the pasta and gently toss to combine with the sauce. Season to taste with salt and black pepper and serve immediately.

Naturally Finnish

LEFT The warmth and cosiness of this interior derives largely from the presence of heavy, dark logs of birch and pine. There is no running water or electricity in the house, so the only sources of artificial light, apart from the fire in the grate, are oil lamps and candles.

ABOVE LEFT An inviting rattan armchair, complete with plump cushions, has been placed in a perfect spot from which to enjoy wide views of the lake.

ABOVE RIGHT This original Pirkka stool was designed by the Finnish interior architect and designer Ilmari Tapiovaara in 1955. It has a seat made of solid stained pine and a frame of lacquered birch.

It would be hard to imagine a more idyllically rustic escape from the stresses of modern life than a cabin on Saimaa, Finland's largest lake, which is like nowhere else on earth, with more than 14,000 islands and a total shoreline measuring more than 15,000 km (9,300 miles). Lake Saimaa is linked to Vyborg on the Gulf of Finland by a major canal that runs through the district of Karelia.

Ritva Puotila, the doyenne of the Finnish textile industry, has hada home on Lake Saimaa for more than 50 years. Ritva came originally from Vyborg, which is now part of Russia. She is steeped in the Karelian culture and its traditional love of ascetism – as is evident in every element of her island retreat. In common with many holiday homes in rural Finland, the property has no electricity or running water. Fresh water has to be brought from the mainland, a short journey away by boat.

Ritva and her husband bought a hectare (2½ acres) of land on the once uninhabited island and built a house there in 1965, since when their property has expanded to include seven separate units, including the original cottage, a kitchen house, a wood-fired sauna and guest accommodation – all of which look as if they had been there for centuries because of the ancient timber used in their construction. The Puotila houses are just yards from the shore of Lake Saimaa, whose shallow water heats up easily in summer.

TOP AND ABOVE The main house is flanked by a long wooden verandah overlooking Lake Saimaa, where an assortment of comfortable chairs offers plenty of opportunity for relaxation. Colourful beach towels and household fabrics are hung up to dry on lines strung between the trees. The ground on the island consists largely of scrubland dotted with rocks and boulders.

THIS PAGE It never gets completely dark in Finland during the summer, so outdoor living continues late into the night. In the Puotila household, most meals are eaten on the deck adjoining the main house, from where there are spectacular views over the lake.

This makes it particularly appealing to swimmers – though hardy people swim in winter too. Fishing and boating are also popular pursuits on the lake.

Since it never gets totally dark here during the summer months, there are many hours in each day to sit out and appreciate the spectacular views, and most meals are taken out in the open. If you are lucky, you might catch sight of a pod of seals playing in the water. Saimaa was once part of the Baltic Sea, and when the lake became cut off at the end of the last ice age, about 7,000 years ago, a population of Baltic seals was left behind. These have developed into a distinct species, known as Saimaa seals.

The most important building in the group – and the one with the thickest walls – is the wood-fired sauna house. Enjoying regular saunas is a long-established ritual in Finland, practised by 99 per cent of the population, and no self-respecting holiday home would be without a sauna cabin, preferably a wood-fired one with no chimney, the oldest and most traditional type. One alternative is an electric sauna, but Finnish

ABOVE AND LEFT A long wooden bench, its cushions covered in colourful striped fabrics, has been built into the outer edge of the deck area. It makes a great place to relax and forget life's troubles. Blue-painted doors with diagonal slats give access to washrooms where, since there is no mains supply, water must be conveyed in buckets.

OPPOSITE A *ryijy* rug made by Ritva adorns the wall behind this dining table – which, at more than 200 years old, is one of the oldest pieces of furniture in the island houses. The table's intricately carved legs recall a primitive artwork. A set of dining chairs with chestnut frames was made in France.

ABOVE A short distance from the main living quarters is the kitchen house, where meals are cooked on an open fire. The fireplace, with its quirky stone chimney, was built by hand and has openings both inside and out.

LEFT A thick crossbeam runs through the centre of the kitchen house, whose interior is even darker than that of the other buildings – blackened by soot from the fireplace. The long bench flanking the table is made entirely of wood with no nails or screws holding it together.

ABOVE Many of the objects on display in the houses are both beautiful and functional. Here, a meticulously carved and decorated model sledge is used for bringing freshly baked loaves to table.

country homes rarely have electricity, and wood-fired saunas are much preferred anyway, since the heat is less dry and the whole experience is felt to be much more authentic. Most people like to spend from 10 to 20 minutes in the hot, humid air and then cool off in a lake or swimming pool before returning to the sauna.

Birch and pine logs from Lapland in northern Finland, greyed by their long exposure to cold and snow, are the main building materials used on the island. Combined with small windows, these robust timbers make for interiors that are dark but restful, where the only light sources are oil lamps, candles and the flames from the wood fires. Much of the furniture dates from the 19th century. The oldest piece is the sturdy 200-year-old dining table in the main house, whose intricate construction gives it the stature of an artwork. And, of course, there are textiles in abundance, ranging from antique Karelian pieces to treasures created by Ritva herself.

RIGHT Four wooden steps lead up to the guest-house door, whose wooden boards are arranged in diamond fashion. Like the rest of the buildings on the island, the guest house was built from birch and pine logs, now worn to a silvery grey.

FAR RIGHT Ritva is emotionally attached to these traditional Sámi boots because they used to belong to her sons when they were children. The upturned toes are typical of the Sámi boots still worn in Lapland today.

BELOW Perhaps the most important building in the group and the one with the thickest walls is the sauna house. Nearly all holiday homes in Finland have their own sauna cabin, preferably a wood-fired one with no chimney, as in this example.

OPPOSITE Birch branches – used by some people to slap their backs in the heat of the sauna – are stored in a bucket on the porch. The wooden scoop is for throwing water on the sauna's hot stones. The rug on the deck was designed by Ritva.

Ritva made her name designing *ryijy* wall rugs – a form of tapestry, unique to Finland, with roots in folk art. 'I see a modern *ryijy* as a painting. Its fuzzy surface is fiercely fascinating and nuanced,' says Ritva, whose innovative approach to textile design dates from childhood. From a young age she won prizes and awards for her work, which included making table textiles for the American firm Dansk.

In 1987, Ritva founded an interior design company called Woodnotes in partnership with her son, Mikko. It grew out of a collaboration with Tampella, the biggest linen producer in Scandinavia at that time, which had given her the idea of using paper yarn in the manufacture of textiles. Since then, Woodnotes has produced, and continues to produce, an enormous range of interior fabrics, from carpets, rugs and blinds to upholstery and small decorative objects. Part of its success stems from the fact that paper yarn produces textiles of completely different quality to those made from other fibres – textiles that are lighter in weight and with more intense colours, for example.

Ritva Puotila is now widely revered not only as a businesswoman but also as a textile artist of the first order. Her works are included in some of the world's most prestigious museums, including the Architecture and Design Collection at the Museum of Modern Art in New York. The action-packed life that results from all this attention makes Ritva value more than ever the peace and solitude offered by the rustic paradise that she and her family have created on the island in Lake Saimaa.

Instead of the usual *béchamel* sauce used to make fish pie, this recipe incorporates another French classic – *soubise* sauce, which is based on white onions. The sweet flavour and firm texture of red snapper makes it an ideal choice for this dish.

Snapper pie

1 tablespoon olive oil

15 g/1 tablespoon butter

900 g/2 lb. (6–7) whole white onions, thinly sliced

2 fresh or dry bay leaves

375 ml/1½ cups fish stock

500 ml/2¼ cups single/light cream

sea salt and freshly ground black pepper

plain/all-purpose flour, for dusting

1 sheet ready-rolled puff pastry, defrosted if frozen

800 g/1¾ lb. red snapper fillets, cut into bite-sized pieces

milk, for glazing

4 individual ovenproof baking dishes, about 10–15 cm/4–6 in. diameter

Serves 4

Heat the olive oil and butter in a heavy-based saucepan set over a medium heat. Add the onions and bay leaves and stir well to break up the onions. Cover and cook for about 30 minutes, stirring often so that the onions sweat and soften. Remove the lid and increase the heat to high. Cook for a further 10 minutes, stirring occasionally so that the onions do not catch and are a pale caramel colour.

Add the fish stock, bring to the boil and cook until the liquid has reduced by half. Reduce the heat to medium and add the cream. Cook for 15 minutes, stirring constantly. Season with salt and pepper. Remove from the heat and let cool. Remove the bay leaves and blend the sauce in a food processor until smooth. Set aside.

Preheat the oven to 220°C (425°F) Gas 7.

Lightly flour a work surface. Roll the pastry out to a thickness of about 2–3 mm/ ⅛ in. Cut 4 circles from the pastry, using an upturned baking dish as a template.

Spoon half the onion sauce into each of the baking dishes. Arrange a quarter of the fish pieces on top, then spoon over the remaining sauce. Repeat to fill all 4 pies. Cover each pie with a pastry circle and press around the edges with the tines of a fork to seal. Use a sharp knife to make 2–3 small incisions in the pastry to let the steam escape. Brush the top of each with a little milk to glaze and bake in the preheated oven for 20–25 minutes, until golden and puffed. Serve with a watercress salad, if liked.

Plants for coastal gardens

Gardening by the sea brings its own particular joys and challenges. Some trees and shrubs look their sculptural best against a coastal backdrop, but in exposed positions they must be able to withstand salt-laden air and drying winds, often combined with poor, free-draining soil. In hot climates, drought resistance is also crucial, as exemplified by the tenacious oleander, which is found throughout the Mediterranean region. Succulents such as aloes and sedums are adapted to store water in their stems and leaves. Aromatic herbs like rosemary, sage and lavender are also good choices for coastal gardens because they grow well in dry conditions in relatively poor soils.

Creating a shelter belt allows you to widen the range of plants that will thrive in an exposed garden. Sea buckthorn, willow and tamarisk are among natural

hedging options. Ground-cover shrubs like creeping thyme and thrift are protected from the wind by their low-growing habit. Choose feather grasses with flexible stems that gracefully bend with the breeze or plants with dramatic foliage such as mountain flax and cordylines.

Plants with grey or silver and downy-textured foliage, including phlomis, ozothamnus and senecio, tend to survive well in salty conditions. Plants with small or narrow leaves such as dianthus and escallonia also withstand salt more easily than those with larger leaves.

Gravel, shingle, crushed shells and organic materials such as seaweed make good mulches in seaside gardens. Mulches not only suppress weeds and reduce water evaporation but also have a decorative purpose. Plants, especially grasses, appear to stand out, their shapes more clearly defined, when planted in an area covered with gravel or shingle.

Sources

UK

Walls and floors

Alternative Flooring
An extensive collection of natural floor coverings, including jute, seagrass, sisal and coir.

Annie Sloan
www.anniesloan.com
Chalk paints for a vintage rustic effect, plus toile de Jouy and patterned, striped and ticking fabrics.

Plantation Shutters
www.plantation-shutters.co.uk
Both MDF and hardwood shutters in a variety of slat sizes.

The Reclaimed Flooring Company
www.reclaimedflooringco.com
Driftwood-effect wood flooring with a naturally weathered effect.

Roger Oates
www.rogeroates.com
Flatweave rugs and runners in smart, simple stripes.

Skandihome
www.skandihome.com
Washable rag rugs in faded seaside hues.

Fabrics and Soft Furnishings

Cabbages and Roses
www.cabbagesandroses.com
Striped and plain fabrics and wallpapers with faded vintage charm.

Cath Kidston
www.cathkidston.com
Affordable fabrics and soft furnishings featuring jaunty retro designs.

Ian Mankin
www.ianmankin.co.uk
Chic striped and ticking fabrics, deckchair canvas and oilcloths.

Vanessa Arbuthnott
www.vanessaarbuthnott.co.uk
Fabrics and wallpapers inspired by the sea.

Furniture and Accessories

Adirondack Outdoors
www.adirondack.co.uk
Adirondack chairs and garden furniture made in the UK and ideal for decks, terraces or coastal locations.

The Beach Hut
www.thebeachhut.com
Home and garden accessories, furniture and soft furnishings for a stylish coastal home.

Buy The Sea
www.buythesea-bymail.co.uk
Online store.
Gifts, art and home accessories inspired by the ocean.

Coastal Home
www.coastalhome.co.uk
Coastal-inspired collection of nautically themed accessories and driftwood art.

Doris by Karen Miller
www.dorisbrixham.co.uk
Driftwood tables, art, sculpture and other coastal-inspired accessories.

Greige
www.greige.co.uk
Storm lanterns and hurricane lamps, handcrafted wooden bowls, driftwood lanterns and home accessories.

Hen & Hammock
www.henandhammock.co.uk
Traditional deckchairs, outdoor furniture and lighting and home accessories.

Jan Constantine
www.janconstantine.com
Distinctive hand-embroidered cushions, some with a nautical theme.

Oceans Rattan Furniture
www.oceansrattanfurniture.com
Wide selection of rattan furniture, for both indoors and out.

Pebbles to Sand
www.pebblestosand.co.uk
Coastal- and nautical-influenced soft furnishings, lighting and accessories.

Seasalt
www.seasaltcornwall.co.uk
Nautical-themed bed linen, towels, pillows, stationery and home fragrance.

Stoves Online
www.stovesonline.co.uk
A wide selection of wood-burning stoves to warm up any coastal home.

Toast
www.toa.st
Relaxed and stylish homewares and soft furnishings for a casual coastal interior.

US

Walls and Floors

American Country
www.americancountryhomestore.com
Braided, natural fibre and hand-knotted rugs, for both indoors and out.

Finnish Design Shop
www.finnishdesignshop.us
Carries textiles and rugs by Ritva Puotila of Woodnotes (see pages 172-181).

Indoteak Design ✓
www.indoteakdesign.com
Flooring, paneling, decking, and other custom products made from enviromentally responsible recycled teak.

Sisal Carpet ✓
www.sisalcarpet.com
Natural sisal floor coverings, runners and rugs plus synthetic sisal for mud rooms, halls and high traffic areas.

Furniture and Accessories

All Posters
www.allposters.com
A good selection of nautical maps and charts plus posters showing assorted knots and vintage lighthouses.

Barn Light Electric ✓
www.barnlightelectric.com
Vintage and industrial style light fixtures.

The Best Adirondack Chair
www.thebestadirondackchair.com
Handcrafted solid wood Adirondack chairs perfect for decks, porches or poolsides.

Coastal Living Boutique ✓
www.wayfair.com/coastalliving
The best in seaside style, chosen by Coastal Living Magazine.

European Sheepskins
www.europeansheepskins.com
Importers of natural sheepskins, including eco-friendly hides. Ideal for warming up bare boards or wicker furniture.

Fishs Eddy
www.fishseddy.com
Casual, relaxed tableware and glassware with a retro twist.

Hammock Universe
www.hammockuniverseusa.com
Rope, fabric and South American-style hammocks for any outdoor setting.

Lexington ✓
www.lexingtoncompany.com
Bed linen and soft furnishings with breezy nautical stripes and checks.

Poster Corner
www.postercorner.com
Vintage and reproduction posters of seaside travel destinations.

Pottery Barn ✓
www.potterybarn.com
Large selection of outdoor furniture including umbrellas, dining tables and outdoor lighting.

Rachel Ashwell Shabby Chic
www.shabbychic.com
Custom machine-washable slipcovered furniture and vintage accessories, along with bedding and other home furnishings. Perfect for a relaxed coastal vibe.

Restoration Hardware ✓
www.restorationhardware.com
Framed maps, reclaimed wood coffee tables, steamer trunks, driftwood chandeliers and natural-fibre rugs plus weathered teak outdoor furniture.

Robert's Maps ✓
www.etsy.com/uk/shop/RobertsMaps
Vintage nautical charts and maps.

Uniquely Nautical ✓
www.uniquelynautical.com
Nautically themed décor and gift ideas, including nautical art, charts and prints.

Wicker Warehouse ✓
www.wickerwarehouse.com
A large selection of outdoor and porch furniture made from natural rattan or synthetic 'All Weather' wicker that can be left outdoors all-year round.

Picture credits

Endpapers ph Paul Massey 1 The home in Denmark of Charlotte Lynggaard, designer of Ole Lynggaard Copenhagen. ph Paul Massey 2–3 Dune House by Stelle Architects, ph Paul Massey 4 A house in the Bahamas designed by Tom Scheerer, ph Paul Massey 5 ph Earl Carter 6 The Cricket Pavilion, designed by David Flint Wood and India Hicks and available for rental from www.hibiscushillharbourisland.com, ph Paul Massey 7 left all items from Côté Jardin boutique in Ars en Ré, France, ph Paul Massey 7 centre ph Paul Massey 7 right Jane Packer's home in Suffolk, ph Paul Massey 8 left The Spreitzer residence, Southampton, New York, ph Paul Massey 8 right ph Jan Baldwin 9 ph Simon Brown 10–11 ph Paul Massey 12–19 Jan Constantine (www.janconstantine.com), ph Paul Massey 20 ph Steve Painter 21 The Barton's seaside home in West Sussex, available for rental at www.thedodo.co.uk, ph Paul Massey 22 above left A house designed by Ilkka Suppanen in Finland, ph Paul Ryan 22 above right ph Paul Massey 22 below right ph Earl Carter 22 below left Nikolay Tzolov/istock 23 Jan Constantine (www.janconstantine.com), ph Paul Massey 23 insert mofles/istock 24–33 Kitchen by Rasmus Larsson, Design by Us, ph Paul Massey 34 ph Earl Carter 36–45 Interior design by Janet Kielley of Janet Kielley Interiors, Architecture by Luke Thornewill of Luke Thornewill Designs, ph Earl Carter 46 ph Steve Painter 47 Crena Watson Photography www.crenawatson.com, ph Earl Carter 48 left ph Earl Carter 48 centre right ph Dan Duchars 48 below right ph Jan Baldwin 49 ph Paul Massey 49 left insert MIGUEL RIOPA/ Stringer/Getty Images 49 right insert Hulton Archive/Handout/ Getty Images 50–59 The Guesthouse and the Cricket Pavilion, designed by David Flint Wood and India Hicks and available for rental from www.hibiscushillharbourisland.com, ph Paul Massey 60 left ph Polly Wreford 60 right ph Paul Massey 61 ph Isobel Wield 62–73 The home of Cary Tamarkin and Mindy Goldberg on Shelter Island, ph Earl Carter 74–75 ph William Reavell 76 Julie Thurston Photography /Getty Images 76 insert Valerie Loiseleux/istock 77 above left © North Wind Picture Archives/Alamy 77 above right © Alpha Historica/Alamy 77 centre right Universal History Archive/Getty Images 77 below right Krysia Campos/Getty Images 77 below left opulent-images/istock 78–87 Surfside by Stelle Architects: a small family compound nestled in the dunes at the water's edge, ph Paul Massey 88 ph Matt Russell 89 ph Earl Carter 90–97 The home of Birgitte and Henrik Møller Kastrup in Denmark, ph Rachel Whiting 98 above left Archive Photos/Getty Images 98 centre right DEA Picture Library/Getty Images 98 below right Ullstein bild/Getty Images 98 below left ph William Lingwood 99 above left DEA Picture Library/Getty Images 99 above right ph Jonathan Gregson 99 below right ph Gavin Kingcome 99 centre left duncan1890/istock 100 The Spreitzer residence, Southampton, New York, ph Paul Massey 101 ph Peter Cassidy 102–103 ph Paul Massey 104–113 The Barton's seaside home in West Sussex, available for rental at www.thedodo.co.uk, ph Paul Massey 114 above right Foster House, available to hire at www.beachstudios.co.uk, ph Polly Wreford 114 below left ph Earl Carter 114 centre left A house in

the Ile de Ré, ph Paul Massey 114 centre right The family home of Hanne Dalsgaard and Henrik Jeppesen in Zealand, Denmark, ph Earl Carter 115 ph Paul Massey 11 left insert Jane Packer's home in Suffolk, ph Paul Massey 115 centre insert The Guesthouse, designed by David Flint Wood and India Hicks and available for rental from www.hibiscushillharbourisland.com, ph Paul Massey 115 right insert Michael Giannelli and Greg Shano's home in East Hampton, ph Paul Massey 116 ph Steve Painter 117 left ph Tom Leighton 117 right ph Steve Painter 118–125 Andrew Hoffman and Alex Bates' home on Fire Island. ph Earl Carter 126 ph Peter Cassidy 127 ph Peter Cassidy 127 insert The Spreitzer residence, Southampton, New York, ph Paul Massey 128–133 Naja Lauf, www.najalauf.dk, ph Paul Massey 134 above left Hôtel Le Sénéchal, Ars en Ré, designed by Christophe Ducharme Architecte, ph Paul Massey 134 centre right all items from Côté Jardin boutique in Ars en Ré, France, ph Paul Massey 134 below right and left Hotel Tresanton, St Mawes, Cornwall, owned and designed by Olga Polizzi, ph Paul Massey 135 above left all items from Côté Jardin boutique in Ars en Ré, France, ph Paul Massey 135 above right Hotel Tresanton, St Mawes, Cornwall, owned and designed by Olga Polizzi, ph Paul Massey 135 below right a house in Cape Elizabeth designed by Stephen Blatt Architects, ph Jan Baldwin 135 centre left and 136 ph Paul Massey 137 ph Peter Cassidy 138–145 A Malibu cottage rental made magical by Rachel Ashwell (www.shabbychic.com), ph Gisela Torres 146–147 ph Paul Massey 148–155 The seaside home of designer Marta Nowicka, available for rental at www.martanowicka.com, ph Rachel Whiting 156–157 ph William Reavell 158 Beauty Point and Coast House, available to hire through www.beachstudios.co.uk, ph Polly Wreford 159 above left ph Mark Scott 159 above right Laurence and Yves Sabourets' house in Brittany, ph Jan Baldwin 159 below right Michael Giannelli and Greg Shano's home in East Hampton, ph Paul Massey 159 centre left ph Francesca Yorke 161 ph Peter Cassidy 162–169 Elena Colombo's cottage on Long Island (www.firefeatures.com), ph Jan Baldwin 170 ph Kate Whitaker 171 The Guesthouse, designed by David Flint Wood and India Hicks and available for rental from www.hibiscushillharbourisland.com. ph Paul Massey 172–181 Ritva Puotila's summerhouse in Finland, ph Paul Ryan 182 ph Kate Whitaker 183 left ph Paul Massey 183 right Elena Colombo's cottage on Long Island (www.firefeatures.com), ph Jan Baldwin 184 above left Marilyn Phipps' house in Kent, ph Tom Leighton 184 above right ph Melanie Eclare 184 centre right Marilyn Phipps' house in Kent, ph Tom Leighton 184 below right ph Jan Baldwin 184 below centre ph Simon Brown 185 above left ph Keiko Oikawa and Amanda Darcy 185 below right Marilyn Phipps' garden in Kent, ph Francesca Yorke 185 below left Kate Whitaker 185 below left ph Paul Massey 185 centre left ph Melanie Eclare 187 Surfside by Stelle Architects: a small family compound nestled in the dunes at the water's edge, ph Paul Massey 189 The home of Cary Tamarkin and Mindy Goldberg on Shelter Island, ph Earl Carter 192 ph Earl Carter.

Index

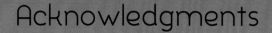

Acknowledgments

The author would like to thank all the owners who allowed us to photograph their beautiful houses, cottages and cabins. Many of them very generously provided information about the design and restoration work involved in creating the home of their dreams, including fascinating insights into the fabric and history of the buildings and the inspirations behind their interior decoration and furnishings.

Warm thanks are due to everyone at Ryland Peters & Small responsible for the editing and design of this book, in particular Annabel Morgan and Toni Kay, and to Christina Borsi and Jess Walton for location research.